FOUNTA  E

Celebrating 150 ... ui Love

Jim McManus C.Ss.R.

redemptorist
p u b l i c a t i o n s

Published by **Redemptorist Publications**
Alphonsus House, Chawton, Hampshire, GU34 3HQ, UK
Tel. +44 (0)1420 88222, Fax. +44 (0)1420 88805
Email rp@rpbooks.co.uk, www.rpbooks.co.uk

A registered charity limited by guarantee
Registered in England 3261721

Copyright © Redemptorist Publications 2015
First published October 2015

Text by Jim McManus C.Ss.R.
Edited by Peter Edwards
Designed by Christine Reissland

ISBN 978-0-85231-437-1

A CIP catalogue record for this book is available from the British Library

Nihil Obstat:
Rev. William Wilson
Censor deputatis

Imprimatur:
+ Rt. Rev. Philip A. Egan BA, STL, PhD
Bishop of Portsmouth
6th October 2015

The *Nihil Obstat* and *Imprimatur* are official declarations that a book or pamphlet is free of doctrinal or moral error. No implication is contained therein that those who have granted the *Nihil Obstat* and *Imprimatur* agree with the contents, opinions or statements expressed.

The publisher gratefully acknowledges permission to use the following copyright material:

Excerpts from THE JERUSALEM BIBLE, copyright © 1966 by Darton, Longman & Todd, Ltd and Doubleday, a division of Random House, Inc. Reprinted by permission.

Excerpts from the documents of the Second Vatican Council are taken from *Vatican Council II: The Basic Sixteen Documents* (Northport, NY: Costello, 1996) © 1996 by Reverend Austin Flannery OP.

Redemptorist Publications are grateful to the Redemptorist General Council in Rome for permission to use the official photo of the restored icon of Our Lady of Perpetual Succour in the church of St Alphonsus, Via Merulana 26, Rome.

Printed by Bishops Printers Limited, Portsmouth PO6 1TR

Other titles by Jim McManus C.Ss.R. available from Redemptorist Publications

The Healing Power of the Sacraments

Healing in the Spirit

Hallowed Be Thy Name

All Generations Will Call Me Blessed

The Inside Job: A Spirituality of True Self-Esteem

I Am My Body: Blessed John Paul's Theology of the Body

Finding Forgiveness: Personal and Spiritual Perspectives
(with Dr Stephanie Thornton)

Searching for Serenity: Spirituality in Later Life
(with Dr Stephanie Thornton)

Going to Mass: Becoming the Eucharist We Celebrate

— Contents —

Foreword

A copy of the icon of Our Lady of Perpetual Succour hangs in my chapel at Archbishop's House. It was given to me by the Redemptorist community in Rome last October when I had the great joy of taking possession of my titular church, San Alfonso, home of the original icon. When I heard San Alfonso was to be my titular church I was delighted because, from my youngest days, devotion to Our Lady of Perpetual Succour has had a special place in my heart.

In our home there was a copy of the icon, a focus of prayer and reassurance. Now as well as in my chapel, I have another copy in my office. Whenever I glance at it I feel secure. I am drawn into the depth of the relationship between Mary and Jesus so beautifully portrayed by the icon.

There is such a depth of compassion in the eyes of the Blessed Mother. She sees me. She knows me. She sees all the suffering of the world and gazes on it with such love and compassion. She sees my anxieties, my small sufferings, and helps me to see them in a true perspective. In the warmth of her compassion, I know I am not alone. I know I can bring my burden to her and leave it with her.

This is so because, in the icon, she already carries all the weight of her son's suffering. In the face of what her child will endure, Mary comforts and supports him, her gaze set profoundly on God's will. "Let it be done to me according to your word." There she finds her peace. There we learn to find ours too.

The icon, then, draws us into the presence of the mystery of suffering in our lives and in our world, a suffering always seen by God, always embraced by God. We learn that no suffering is pointless because it is swept up into the divine providence that shapes the life of each of us. There it becomes part of God's redemptive plan. Something of the depth of God, something of his greatness, is opened for us through the icon. We see the angels, messengers of God himself, bringing forward the symbols of the Lord's passion and death with dignity and majesty. This is not random evil, arbitrary pain, pointless suffering. No, they are carried towards Jesus for his willing acceptance and highest purpose. In their light we begin to glimpse that he is no ordinary child who will come to a sad end. Rather he is fully God, uniquely one with the Father and the Holy Spirit in the divine nature: yet also fully one of us. He is true God and true man. Through the instruments of his passion, he transforms our fallen mortal nature, bringing us to share in his own divine nature.

Thus the icon helps us to find our place in God's great mystery of salvation. It enables us to see the almost incredible: that through our suffering and pain, whatever form it may take, we can become part of this great work of Jesus. We can unite our sufferings with his and offer them to the Father. They can become a profound achievement, for through our suffering we can be shaped more completely for God's purpose, purified for his desire. And that desire, that purpose is that we come into his presence, totally filled with his light and joy. As we are emptied of self, we are ready to be filled with God.

So I see this blessed icon as an antidote to the shallowness of our lives and of so many aspects of our times. So often we flee pain and go to great lengths to obliterate it from our lives. Here we learn a new and startling way from our Blessed Mother and her divine son. So often we hide from God, turning away, turning towards passing pleasure in order to mask our need and redirect our emptiness away from the one source that truly meets and fills it. So often we fail to invite this child, Jesus, to walk with us, preferring to struggle on by ourselves, sometimes rejoicing in great love and friendship, sometimes feeling desolate and alone. Yet he wants to walk with us on every path, on the pathway of our joy and love, on the pathway of our desolation and loneliness. He looks out towards us with longing in his eyes. He longs to be with us and for us to be with him.

Our Lady of Unfailing Help is there, offering him to us, that we may discover afresh the true depth of our living and our loving, of our servings and our suffering. Under her guidance we find the way again. With her we can bring so many others to walk this same path and receive this same consolation. This is the great mission we receive from the icon of Our Lady of Perpetual Succour, or the "Icon of Love" as this book aptly names it.

I very much welcome this excellent publication by Fr Jim McManus as we near the 150th anniversary of the icon being entrusted into the care of the Redemptorists in Rome. My prayer is that it will inspire many more people to discover the power of devotion to Our Lady of Perpetual Succour and so, like me, and millions of others, be touched by the infinite love and mercy of her son.

✝ Vincent Nichols

Cardinal Vincent Nichols,
Archbishop of Westminster
Solemnity of St Joseph, Husband of the Blessed Virgin Mary, 2015

Introduction

On 26 April 1866 a providential fountain of grace was opened for the universal Church when the miraculous icon of Our Lady of Perpetual Succour was solemnly enshrined in the Redemptorist church of St Alphonsus in Rome. Ever since then the cleansing, sanctifying and fortifying flow of grace from Our Lady's shrine has washed over the whole Church, bringing conversion to hardened sinners, health and wholeness to those who are suffering and broken-hearted, inspiration and holiness to great saints like St Thérèse of Lisieux and St John Paul II, and comfort and consolation to all the faithful who invoke her powerful intercession. The miraculous icon has truly been the "Icon of Love", beaming the love of God, the love of Jesus and Our Lady's own love into hearts that are open to receive.

As we approach the 150th anniversary of the entrusting of the miraculous icon of Our Lady of Perpetual Succour to the guardianship of the Redemptorists in Rome, it is fitting that we retell the story of how the icon came to be entrusted to the Redemptorists, and also that we remember the phenomenal spread of devotion to Our Lady of Perpetual Succour in the past 150 years. From being unknown to the Catholic world in 1865 this icon of Our Lady has become the most widely known, reverenced and loved image of Our Lady of all time. In this book I will tell the story of how Our Lady herself willed that her Icon of Love be placed in the church of St Alphonsus in Rome and how she has poured out amazing blessings on those who put their love and trust in her.

In the first chapter we will discover how the miraculous icon came, in the first place, to the church of St Alphonsus in Rome. It is a remarkable story of how divine providence prevails, and how what often seems to be the end turns out to be, by God's design, a new beginning.

The second chapter will describe in some detail the phenomenal spread of devotion to Our Mother of Perpetual Succour throughout the Church. Dioceses were placed under her protection; hundreds of churches were dedicated to her; reproductions of her miraculous icon were made in their tens of thousands; in the homes of millions of Catholic families the picture of Our Mother of Perpetual Succour had an honoured place.

In the third chapter we will look at the development of the Perpetual Novena as an innovative, pastoral way of organising and developing on a parish or city level this powerful devotion to Our Mother of Perpetual Succour. This novena still takes place each week in seventy-one countries of the world. That, in itself, is an amazing religious phenomenon.

In the fourth chapter we will consider the need for new forms of the Perpetual Novena to preserve and promote the devotion to Our Mother of Perpetual Succour in our own times. In some parishes and cities in Britain and other countries today the Perpetual Novena is not celebrated. What can take its place?

The fifth chapter will look at the "Icon of Love" itself. We will "read" the icon and allow ourselves to be drawn into the mystery of God's love and compassion that it portrays.

In the sixth chapter we will discuss the theological basis for our belief in the powerful intercession of Our Mother of Perpetual Succour. This will give us the opportunity to discuss in some detail the Church's teaching on Mary's role in the work of our salvation.

In the appendix to the book is the format of the Perpetual Novena that is widely used today. You may find these prayers of the novena helpful as you join with Christians all over the world in celebrating this great jubilee of the 150th anniversary. It will be a year-long festival of prayer. We will be giving thanks to God for the gift of the Icon of Love that has been such a fountain of grace for the whole Church. And we will also be praying for the renewal of devotion to Our Mother of Perpetual Succour at home and abroad. Our Church and our world stand in great need today of her powerful protection and intercession.

This is our special Jubilee prayer to Our Mother of Perpetual Succour:

> O Mother of Perpetual Succour,
> Icon of Love,
> your compassionate gaze
> at our suffering, and that of Jesus,
> entrusts us into the love of the Father.
>
> Help us to make you known even more,
> and to be missionaries
> of the good, beautiful and
> joyful life of the Gospel.
> Open our hearts
> to the cry of those without hope
> until all come to believe.
>
> Teach us to ponder the Word in our heart
> and to do what your son, our Redeemer,
> asks us to do.
> Help us to walk with you,
> with the great light of faith
> to illumine our path.
>
> Thus, one day, we will be able
> to contemplate with you
> the face of the Father

who with the Son and Holy Spirit
lives and reigns for ever and ever.
Amen.

Many people offered me great help and encouragement in writing this book. My confrère Fr Charles Corrigan read the manuscript and made some very helpful suggestions which I acted on. I had the unfailing and prayerful support of my community throughout the time of writing. My family and my lay and religious friends have been a constant source of encouragement and inspiration to me. I am very grateful to all. I offer a special word of thanks to Cardinal Vincent Nichols, the Archbishop of Westminster, who has taken the time to write the Foreword in which he shares with us his own great devotion to Our Mother of Perpetual Succour.

Fr Jim McManus C.Ss.R.

— Chapter 1 —

From Crete to Rome

The miraculous icon of Our Lady of Perpetual Succour had a long and illustrious history before the Redemptorists received it in 1866. We know that it was venerated on the island of Crete in the fifteenth century and was acclaimed as miraculous. The small island of Crete became the refuge for many artists and iconographers who had to flee from the Turkish invasions. The Turkish forces eventually captured Constantinople in 1453. "Crete became the new centre for Byzantine art."[1] An unknown Cretan iconographer, most likely a monk, wrote the miraculous icon. And we know that it vanished from Crete, around the year 1498, and a year later it was being venerated in the church of St Matthew in Rome.

The story of how it got from Crete to Rome is worth telling. A merchant, who was sailing from Crete to Rome, stole the icon and hid it in his luggage as he boarded the ship. How the icon that the merchant stole came to be in St Matthew's church in Rome in 1499 is recounted in a contemporary history that was printed on parchment, in both Latin and Italian, and hung for many years in the choir of St Matthew's. It is now in the Vatican Museum. "This document gives the history of the arrival of the picture in Rome and its solemn enthronement in the Augustinian church of St Matthew."[2] It also records Our Lady's interventions to ensure that the icon was placed in the church of her choice.

On the voyage to Rome, according to the document that recorded this history, a violent storm burst around the ship and it was in grave danger of being shipwrecked. The sailors fervently implored

---

1   Fabriciano Ferrero C.Ss.R., *The Story of an Icon* (Chawton: Redemptorist Publications, 2001), p. 38.
2   R.J. Spitzer C.Ss.R., *The Miraculous Image of Our Mother of Perpetual Help* (Liguori, 1954), p. 20.

14

the intercession of Our Lady; the storm abated; the ship was saved and reached the port. When the merchant arrived in Rome he fell seriously ill. Realising that he was at the point of death, he told a friend his story of stealing the icon and said, "I therefore entreat you, now that my imminent death prevents me from taking it to the place I intended, to bring it to the church most fitting for the image."[3] The man promised his dying friend that he would fulfil his last wish. But there were complications. When the beautiful icon was found in the dead man's luggage the friend's wife became so fascinated with it that she refused to allow her husband to give it to a church. She hung it in her bedroom. The document records that her husband was warned twice in vivid dreams that Our Lady wanted the picture placed in a church. But he refused to act. Our Lady appeared to him again in a dream and gave him a solemn warning that he had to place the icon in a church. Again he refused to act. The document records,

> The Roman then fell ill and died. Some time later the Virgin appeared to his six-year-old daughter and said to her: "Give this message to your mother and to your grandfather: Holy Mary of Perpetual Help requires that you remove her from your house, if not, you will all soon die". The girl told her mother of the vision and the mother then became fearful because she too had had the same vision.[4]

It was Our Lady herself, according to this tradition, who named the icon "Our Mother of Perpetual Succour".[5] The girl's mother still resisted parting with the icon.

> Finally, the glorious Virgin appeared again to the little girl and told her to tell her mother that the image must be placed between St Mary Major and St John Lateran, in a church dedicated to the apostle Matthew. Her mother obeyed and, having advised the friars of St Augustine at this church, with the help of the clergy and all the people, the image

---

3   Ferrero, *Story of an Icon*, p. 132.
4   Ferrero, *Story of an Icon*, p. 133.
5   George Wadding C.Ss.R., *Reflections on an Icon* (Dublin: Redemptorist Communications, 2014), p. 3.

was taken there and on the very day of its removal the first miracle occurred; an individual totally paralysed in the right arm and side was suddenly freed from his ailment after simply commending himself to God and the Virgin and making a promise.[6]

The icon of Our Mother of Perpetual Succour was venerated for nearly three hundred years in the church of St Matthew. Throughout those years many pilgrims to Rome, as well as many local people, came to pray before the icon, imploring Our Lady's intercession. Many received miraculous answers to their prayer, which they attributed to the powerful intercession of Our Mother of Perpetual Succour.

Shrine of the miraculous icon demolished

From 1739 to 1798 the priests in charge of St Matthew's church were Irish Augustinians. They had sought refuge in Rome at a time of severe persecution of the Catholic Church in Ireland. During their sixty years in charge of the church they witnessed the great devotion of the local people and the many pilgrims who flocked to pray before the miraculous icon. But war came to Rome in 1798. Napoleon Bonaparte's victorious army entered the city. The following year thirty churches in Rome, including St Matthew's, were demolished. The Augustinians had to seek refuge in the small monastery of St Mary in Posterula near the River Tiber. They brought the miraculous icon with them, but they had to place it in their private chapel, because for centuries the picture of Our Lady of Grace had the place of honour in their new church. Gradually, as the community members changed, the icon was forgotten about.

People presumed that the miraculous icon had perished in the destruction of the church of St Matthew, which was levelled to the ground. In 1801 Pius VII described the destruction of St Matthew's:

---

6   Ferrero, *Story of An Icon*, p. 133.

"The Church of San Matteo was so utterly uprooted from its very foundations that not only was worship in it discontinued but hardly the slightest vestige of it could be found."[7]

Our Lady intervenes

Fifty years later the derelict site of St Matthew's church was found by Fr Edward Douglas, a Scottish Redemptorist, who had been commissioned by his superior to find a place in Rome where the Redemptorists could build their international headquarters. Fr Douglas, the son of a Scottish nobleman, a convert to the Catholic Church from the Anglican Oxford Movement, had become a Redemptorist in 1849. He was a friend of Blessed John Henry Newman, who had become a Catholic around the same time.

In 1853 Blessed Pius IX told the Redemptorist Vicar General, Fr Rudolph von Smetana, who, at the time, resided at Altötting in Bavaria, to establish a general house in Rome and call a general chapter so that the governance of the expanding Congregation could be centralised. Fr Von Smetana, a saintly man, now had a big problem: he had no money for such a major development. When Fr Douglas heard about this command of Pius IX and the financial problem it posed to the Vicar General, he offered to cover the cost.[8] He had received a large inheritance from his wealthy family on the death of his mother and was making it all available for the needs of the Congregation. On receiving this good news of financial support, the Vicar General wrote to Fr Douglas, who at the time was preaching a parish mission with five other Redemptorists in Strabane in the north of Ireland, asking him to come as soon as possible and meet with him in Altötting. Douglas departed immediately for Bavaria. He spent some days with Fr Von Smetana discussing the kind of property that was needed as the international headquarters for the Congregation in Rome.

7   Spitzer, *Miraculous Image*, p. 31
8   George Stebbing C.Ss.R., *Father Edward Douglas, C.Ss.R. (1819–1898)* (London: Catholic Truth Society, 1917), p. 13. Twelve years before Fr Douglas died in 1898, Fr George Stebbing was ordained as a Redemptorist priest in England. He would have been very familiar with the life and work of Fr Douglas, who also joined the Redemptorists in England and who remained in close contact with the Redemptorist communities in England and Scotland during all his years in Rome.

17

The Vicar General then entrusted the whole project to Fr Douglas and sent him to Rome with the authority to find a suitable property. Fr Douglas searched all over Rome for a good property. A number of convents and monasteries were available, but Fr Douglas, providentially as it turned out, did not accept any of them and kept looking. Eventually he found what he was looking for. A large property known as the Villa Caserta, quite close to St Mary Major on the Via Merulana, came on the market. This was an extensive property including fourteen acres of gardens, with a large manor house at the centre. The large house was in fairly good condition and there was plenty of space for the new church in honour of St Alphonsus. Fr Douglas bought the whole site in 1855 at a cost of £10,000 from his family inheritance. Without being aware of the historic significance of the purchase, he had actually bought the site on which the destroyed church of St Matthew stood for hundreds of years. As one researcher writes, "The church would have occupied a position in what was now assigned as a vegetable garden on the property of the Villa Caserta."[9] After some adaptations to the building, a small group of Redemptorists established their international community in Rome on 26 April 1856. Fr Douglas was appointed Rector. Their first task was to prepare for the general chapter that Pius IX had decreed. During the general chapter a young French Redemptorist, Fr Nicholas Mauron, was elected Superior General and Fr Douglas was elected as one of his six consultors.

After the general chapter Fr Douglas began to organise the building of the church of St Alphonsus Liguori, the founder of the Redemptorists. This church was completed and consecrated on 3 May 1859. On the following day Pius IX made an unofficial visit to the new church of St Alphonsus and met the community.[10]

---

9   Adelino M. Garcia Paz, *Holy Mary of Perpetual Help*, vol. I: *History and Interpretation of the Icon* (Singapore: Redemptorist Community, 1991), p. 39.
10 Garcia Paz, *Holy Mary of Perpetual Help*, vol. I, p. 38.

A hidden treasure

The Redemptorist community, in their new monastery, were getting on with their daily life and ministry, unaware that the new property held any great secrets. Then, one day in 1862, the house chronicler read accounts of the miraculous icon of Our Lady that had been venerated for centuries in a church that must have stood within the grounds of their monastery. Naturally this excited the curiosity of the community. What had happened to the church and what had happened to the famous icon?

The new church of St Alphonsus, built on the site of the destroyed church of St Matthew, was now the church "between the two great basilicas of St John Lateran and Mary Major". But the significance of this fact didn't dawn on the community because they didn't know the history of the miraculous icon and how it came to be venerated in the old St Matthew's. What had happened to the icon? Had it been destroyed when the church was destroyed? Had somebody rescued it, and was it located in some convent or monastery in Rome?

Nobody knew where the miraculous icon was. It was assumed that it had been destroyed when St Matthew's church was destroyed. Then Our Lady herself let it be known where it was. A young man by the name of Michael Marchi was the first novice to join the Redemptorists in Rome in 1855. He was ordained a priest in 1859. As a boy he had served Mass in the private chapel of St Mary in Posterula where the Irish Augustinians had taken refuge after the destruction of their monastery and church of St Matthew. An old Augustinian lay Brother, Brother Augustine Orsetti, who had lived in the community of St Matthew and knew its history well, frequently pointed to the picture of Our Lady in the private chapel and impressed on the young Michael that it was the miraculous icon of Our Mother of Perpetual Succour and should be in a church for public veneration. Writing about his conversations with Brother Augustine, Fr Marchi recalled:

This good Brother always repeated to me in a certain mysterious way and with some anxiety specially in 1850 and 1852, these precise words: "You should know, my Little Michael, that the Virgin of St Matthew is the one which is in the chapel up there, do not forget it. It is certain, certain, dear Michael. Have you understood? It was a miraculous picture". At that time this Brother was nearly completely blind.[11]

Now, as a young Redemptorist priest, when he heard his confrères talk about the famous picture and how it was lost or destroyed, he was able to say that he knew where it was. He would retell the story of how Brother Augustine impressed on him as a boy that the icon in the private chapel of the Augustinians was the famous miraculous picture and that it should be in a public church where it would be venerated by the people.

During 1863 a Jesuit preacher, Fr Francis Blosi, an expert on Marian shrines and pictures, speaking to a vast audience about famous pictures of Our Lady in Rome, mentioned Our Lady of Perpetual Succour. He appealed for information about the whereabouts of this miraculous icon. He said that if anyone knew where the icon was, he or she had a duty to make it known because that picture had to be, at Our Lady's own request, in the church that "stood between the two great basilicas". Needless to say this talk had a profound impact on the community. That was their new church of St Alphonsus!

Fr Marchi knew where the holy icon was but he didn't know where Our Lady wanted it to be. Now the community began to realise that their church should be the new shrine of the miraculous icon. They told the Superior General, Fr Nicholas Mauron, about Fr Blosi's appeal and about Fr Michael Marchi's knowledge of where the picture was. Fr Mauron requested further information from Fr Blosi.

---

11 Garcia Paz, *Holy Mary of Perpetual Help*, vol. I, p. 34.

The Jesuit kindly sent him a copy of his talk and informed him that he read about the picture in a book published in 1729.

Fr Mauron now knew the history of the miraculous icon. He knew that it should be in the new church of St Alphonsus. But he didn't rush to claim it for his church. Instead he asked his confrères to begin a period of special prayer for guidance. They kept this intention in their prayers for three years.

Audience with Blessed Pope Pius IX

Fr Mauron, with Fr Michael Marchi, sought an audience with Blessed Pius IX. He received them on 11 December 1865. Fr Mauron presented him with a written report and Fr Michael was able to tell him how he had seen the miraculous icon and how Brother Augustine had explained to him that it was the picture of Our Mother of Perpetual Succour. Having heard the story of how the icon came to be in a private chapel, Pius IX wrote, on the back of the report, in his own hand:

11 December 1865

The Cardinal Prefect of Propaganda will summon the Superior of the community of Santa Maria in Posterula and will tell him that it is our wish that the image of the Most Holy Mary, to which this report relates, should return to its position between St John Lateran and St Mary Major; and that the Liguorians (the Redemptorists) should provide the community with another suitable painting in its place.[12]

The Irish Augustinian Prior of Santa Maria, Fr Jeremias O'Brien, in accordance with the Pope's wishes, visited Fr Mauron and negotiated the handover of the sacred icon. His visit is recorded in the Redemptorist chronicles in Rome:

---

12 Ferrero, *Story of an Icon*, p. 110.

Yesterday, 18th of January 1866, after lunch, the Prior of St Mary in Posterula came to talk to Fr General; he declared to him that he willingly transferred the image, but due to the poverty of his convent, he hoped that beside the second image according to the direction of the Pope, some financial assistance might be extended.

Fr Mauron and Fr O'Brien quickly reached an amicable agreement. The Redemptorist chronicle for the following day records:

Today, the 19th of January, after lunch Fathers Bresciani and Marchi went to Santa Maria in Posterula bringing 50 escudos for the Prior together with a letter from Father General. Fr Prior accepted the above-mentioned sum as a donation, and delivered to the Fathers the image which was brought immediately to the house, where it was welcomed with great joy by the community.[13]

New shrine of Our Lady of Perpetual Succour

Before the miraculous icon was enshrined in the church of St Alphonsus it needed extensive restoration. This was carried out by a Polish artist. The Cardinal Vicar of Rome then invited all the faithful to join in a solemn procession on 26 April 1866 as the icon of Our Lady of Perpetual Succour was being brought to its new shrine. It was a very joyful event, attended by large numbers of people. A Roman newspaper, *Giornale di Roma*, described the event:

The solemnities announced for the restoration to public veneration of the image of Most Holy Mary under the title of Perpetual Succour, took place at the days mentioned. The enthusiasm and the manifestation of solid and deep fervour surpassed all expectations.[14]

As the procession passed by a house where a mother was nursing her very sick four-year-old son, she brought him to the window and

---

13 Garcia Paz, *Holy Mary of Perpetual Help*, vol. I, p. 48.
14 Garcia Paz, *Holy Mary of Perpetual Help*, vol. I, p. 53.

cried out, "O good Mother, either cure my child or take him with you to Paradise!" Within a few days the boy was completely restored to health. Other miraculous healings happened and within days the church of St Alphonsus began to attract many visitors who wanted to pray before the miraculous picture.

Blessed Pius IX himself visited the new shrine on 5 May 1866, just nine days after the icon was enshrined in the church of St Alphonsus. The Redemptorist chronicler relates:

> He knelt in the middle of the sanctuary and prayed for a while with great fervour visible to all, to the Virgin of Perpetual Succour, as before he had prayed when a child, in the church of St Matthew, as he related to Most Reverend Father General.[15]

This was the first time that the Pope had revealed his childhood connections with the miraculous icon in the old church of St Matthew. He was born in 1792 and the church was destroyed in 1798. He would have been about six years old when the church was demolished. So he would have had a good childhood memory of the old church and its famous icon of Our Lady of Perpetual Succour. On the occasion of his visit Blessed Pius IX gave the Redemptorists the mandate "to make her known to the world". It was as if he had said, "I have given you the icon – now you make Our Lady of Perpetual Succour known to the whole world."

The faithful of the local neighbourhood of the church of St Alphonsus wanted their own celebration of thanksgiving. The miraculous icon that their ancestors had venerated for three hundred years in the church of St Matthew had returned to them. They wanted "to organize something which would surpass even the celebrations of the inauguration".[16] Responding to their requests, the Cardinal Vicar of Rome announced that a special three days, a Triduum, of thanksgiving would be held on 1 to 3 June, just five weeks after the

15 Garcia Paz, *Holy Mary of Perpetual Help*, vol. I, p. 58.
16 Garcia Paz, *Holy Mary of Perpetual Help*, vol. I, p. 59.

solemn installation of the icon. He said to the people: "We exhort you with our whole heart to emulate the devotion which, during three centuries, our forefathers had for this beloved image, when it was exposed in the destroyed Church of St Matthew."[17] Once again, great numbers took part in all the services of thanksgiving. The people of Rome had become aware of the presence of the miraculous icon in their city. Hundreds flocked to the church of St Alphonsus to pray before the shrine of Our Lady of Perpetual Succour.

---

17 Garcia Paz, *Holy Mary of Perpetual Help*, vol. I, p. 60.

— Chapter 2 —

The fountain begins to overflow

Such was the enthusiasm and fervour of the people that Fr Nicholas Mauron, the Superior General of the Redemptorists, and the local parish priests proposed that the icon should be crowned. Only very ancient pictures of Our Lady that were publicly venerated and believed to be miraculous were solemnly crowned. As the icon of Our Lady of Perpetual Succour was ancient, deeply revered by the people and held to be miraculous, the Vatican Chapter, responsible for such a decision, accepted the proposal and on 12 May 1867 the Chapter issued the decree of crowning. On the same day the Cardinal Vicar of Rome published an invitation to all the people of Rome to participate in the joyful celebrations. This was the third time within twelve months that the Cardinal Vicar had invited the people to come to the church of St Alphonsus to honour Our Lady of Perpetual Succour. There would be seven days of religious feasts: three days in preparation, the day of the solemn crowning and three days of thanksgiving. The central event of the crowning would take place on Sunday 23 June 1867.[1]

Eighteenth centenary of the martyrdom of St Peter and St Paul

Providentially the time of the celebrations for the crowning of the icon coincided with the eighteenth centenary of the martyrdom of St Peter and St Paul. An estimated five hundred bishops from around the world, with hundreds of priests and many thousands of faithful, were in Rome for this great celebration. Many of them attended the ceremony of the solemn crowning of the icon. With the attendance

---

1   Adelino M. Garcia Paz, *Holy Mary of Perpetual Help*, vol. I: *History and Interpretation of the Icon* (Singapore: Redemptorist Community, 1991), p. 62.

of so many bishops, the Redemptorist chronicler could record, "The feast of the crowning surpassed all those which till that moment had been celebrated in honour of Perpetual Succour."[2] Remarkably, within the space of a year, hundreds of bishops, priests and faithful from all over the world had their own personal experience of the power of devotion to Our Lady of Perpetual Succour. When those bishops and priests returned to their dioceses and parishes they were eager to promote this devotion. As we have seen in the previous chapter, Blessed Pius IX gave the Redemptorists the mission "to make her known to the whole world". As the Redemptorists had already established missions in many countries, bishops and priests who had experienced the crowning of the icon were very happy to invite them to preach parish missions and promote devotion to Our Lady of Perpetual Succour.

First Vatican Council, 1869–1870

Two years after the crowning of the icon another major international religious event began in Rome; what we now know as the First Vatican Council. Many of the bishops who had been in Rome for the eighteenth centenary of the martyrdom of St Peter and St Paul, and who experienced the festivities of the crowning of the icon, were now back in Rome for many months of deliberations. Bishops who had not visited Rome for the great celebration now had the opportunity of experiencing for themselves the power of devotion to Our Lady of Perpetual Succour and the beauty and attraction of the miraculous icon. Some of the bishops were lodged with the Redemptorists during their time at the Vatican Council and would have prayed every day before the shrine. Many bishops gathered frequently in the Redemptorist house to discuss the issues being raised in the Council, and they would also have prayed before the shrine in the church of St Alphonsus.

---

2   Garcia Paz, *Holy Mary of Perpetual Help*, vol. I, p. 65.

In God's providence, within the space of three years, an icon that was unknown to the bishops of the Church had become known to so many of them. It was as if Our Lady had delayed the restoration of her icon to "the church between the two great basilicas of St Mary Major and St John Lateran" until these great international events, the eighteenth centenary of the martyrdom of St Peter and St Paul and the First Vatican Council, brought bishops, priests and hundreds of thousands of lay men and women from around the world to Rome. The German bishop William Emmanuel Kettler, a great social reformer of the nineteenth century, returned to his diocese after the Council with a copy of the icon. He had personally experienced the great devotion of the people who visited the church of St Alphonsus and heard reports from others of the many graces that people in different parts of the world were receiving through their devotion to Our Mother of Perpetual Succour. He wrote to the people of his diocese:

> An extraordinary devotion and a marvellous confidence in the powerful intercession of the Mother of God towards all our needs has been aroused in the faithful everywhere. Graces similar to those obtained in Rome are obtained everywhere. It may be stated that soon there will be no place where the venerable image of the Virgin of Perpetual Succour is not exposed. What better gift than an image of the Virgin of Perpetual Succour could I have brought for you, who love the most Holy Mother of God so much.[3]

Our Lady of Perpetual Succour protects her new shrine in Rome

The First Vatican Council ended abruptly. The Papal States, governed by the Pope for many centuries, were invaded by Italian nationalist forces. Rome was surrendered on 20 September 1870 and the small army of papal soldiers was disbanded. Blessed Pius IX

---

3   Garcia Paz, *Holy Mary of Perpetual Help*, vol. I, p. 66.

withdrew to the Vatican. The nationalists' dream of the unification of Italy had been achieved. The Italian Government now began the confiscation of a great number of ecclesiastical properties. Fr Edward Douglas flew the British flag from the house in an attempt to save the Redemptorist community house, known as the College of St Alphonsus, from confiscation. The deeds of the whole property were made out in his name. He sent the deeds to the British ambassador, claiming that since the property belonged to him, as a British citizen, the British Government should protect the house, the church and the gardens. The ambassador sent the deeds on to the Foreign Office in London. The Foreign Office rejected Fr Douglas' claim and declared that the estate made out in his name did not count as British property. Fr Douglas was also instructed to take down the British flag.[4]

Undeterred, Fr Douglas now had recourse to the Italian courts. The Villa Caserta property was sold to a British national and the College of St Alphonsus was established as an international college. But the decision in the court also went against him. The property could be confiscated according to Italian law. The situation was grim. Would the Redemptorists lose the entire property? No doubt Fr Douglas and the whole community put all their trust in Our Mother of Perpetual Succour. And she did not fail them. A Polish lady, the wife of the French ambassador, the Marquis de Noailles, had arrived in Rome as her husband had been transferred from Washington. Before she left Washington, a very close friend begged her to go to the church of St Alphonsus and say a special prayer for her before the miraculous icon of Our Lady of Perpetual Succour. She promised her friend that as soon as she got to Rome she would visit the shrine. She was so deeply impressed by the experience of praying before the miraculous icon that she asked to see the Superior of the house. Fr Mauron, a Frenchman himself, welcomed her. She wanted to hear the full story of the miraculous icon. Fr Mauron gave her the history and then explained the serious legal situation that put the whole establishment

---

4   George Stebbing C.Ss.R., *Father Edward Douglas C.Ss.R. (1819–1898)* (London: Catholic Truth Society, 1917), p. 24.

at risk of being confiscated by the Italian Government. He impressed on her that this would be a terrible injustice to Fr Douglas, whose rights to the property were not recognised. He asked her if she could use her influence as the wife of the new French ambassador to help the Redemptorist community maintain their college and church. The Marchioness de Noailles promised that she would. She began her own diplomatic campaign. Fr George Stebbing writes,

> She approached the Italian Royal Ministers as well as the British Ambassador and others, and she did it with such good purpose that though the Tribunal of Appeal had already given an unfavourable decision a new hearing was ordered by the Council of State. The result of this was that, against all expectations, the Council, influenced by what the Marchioness de Noailles had urged, and there is reason to believe after the expression of a wish on the part of King Victor Emmanuel himself, decided that the College of the Redemptorists had been validly set up as a corporate body of international character, and hence the property was exempt from the general decree of suppression. Furthermore, that as the garden had already been seized for the purpose of making improvements and erecting new houses in the district, some compensation should be paid for what had been taken. This decree of the Council of State bears the date the 19th of June, 1879, and ever since the community has remained in peaceful possession of both house and church.[5]

Our Lady very often answers prayer by sending the right person to deal with the situation. In this perilous moment in which the Redemptorists could have lost both their college and their church, with its shrine to Our Mother of Perpetual Succour, the right person arrived when the Marchioness de Noailles knelt and prayed before the icon. This miracle was worked for the whole Redemptorist Congregation and,

---

5   Stebbing, *Father Edward Douglas*, p. 25.

indeed, for the whole Church, which was about to receive so many graces from devotion to Our Lady of Perpetual Succour.

Redemptorist community in Liverpool

Fr Edward Douglas, who became a Redemptorist in London, was, as we have seen, in God's providence, the person who by purchasing the "treasure hidden in the vegetable garden" of the Villa Caserta, namely, the ruins of St Matthew's church, brought the miraculous icon out of obscurity in that private chapel in St Mary in Posterula to its new shrine in the beautiful new church of St Alphonsus. He was the Rector when the miraculous icon was brought to the community on 19 January 1866. In February of that year, Fr Lammens C.Ss.R., who had been on a visit to Fr Douglas, set out from Rome and arrived in the Redemptorist community known as Bishop Eton in Liverpool. He told the community about Blessed Pius IX entrusting the miraculous icon of Our Lady of Perpetual Succour to the new church of St Alphonsus. When the community heard about the miraculous icon they began a novena to Our Mother of Perpetual Succour for one of their members, Fr Hall, who was seriously ill. At the end of the novena his condition seemed worse, so they started another novena. Fr William Raemers writes,

> Wonderful to say, the next morning, the priest was instantaneously cured. As the Angelus bell rang at 6.00am, a change came over him and he joyfully exclaimed: "I feel as if new life has been infused into my body". In the archives of the house of Bishop Eton, dated 2nd March 1866, we read, "Today the house of Bishop Eton was filled with joy and gratitude at the miraculous cure of Rev. Fr Hall, through the intercession of the Madonna of Perpetual Succour."[6]

This miraculous cure happened even before the icon had been solemnly enshrined in the church of St Alphonsus on 26 April 1866.

---

6   William Raemers C.Ss.R., *The Mother of Perpetual Succour* (London: Catholic Truth Society, 1939), p. 17.

The Rector of the Bishop Eton community wrote to Fr Mauron in Rome, informing him of the miraculous healing of Fr Hall and requesting a copy of the miraculous icon. Fr Raemers writes,

> The Most Rev. Fr Mauron C.Ss.R. was so struck by Fr Hall's sudden recovery that he sent the second copy of the picture to Liverpool.[7] Thus, to England, Our Lady's Dowry, belongs the unique privilege of possessing the FIRST COPY to leave Rome.[8]

Since the Redemptorist community in Liverpool began their novena in February 1866, two months before the icon was enshrined and became known in Rome on 26 April 1866, they are most likely to have been the first community in the whole Church to have made a novena to Our Mother of Perpetual Succour for the healing of a sick member. The Redemptorist church in Liverpool became the first shrine of Our Mother of Perpetual Succour in England.

First diocese in the world to be dedicated to Our Lady of Perpetual Succour

Among the multitudes taking part in the solemn and joyful procession bringing the miraculous icon to the church of St Alphonsus was an Irish seminarian, Richard Lacy, who was preparing for the priesthood at the English College in Rome. He was ordained a priest in 1867. He wrote,

> I was fortunate enough to witness the glorious procession in which the picture of Our Lady of Perpetual Succour was, for the first time borne [to] the Church of St Alphonsus through the streets of Rome: it was a sight never to be forgotten, and made a deep impression on my mind, which time has not obliterated.[9]

A year after the Diocese of Middlesbrough was created in 1878, Fr Richard Lacy was appointed its first bishop on 12 September 1879.

---

7   The first copy of the icon was presented to Blessed Pius IX.
8   Raemers, *Mother of Perpetual Succour*, p. 17.
9   Cornelia R. Ferreira, *Bishop Lacy and Our Lady of Perpetual Succour* <http://canisiusbooks.com/bishop_lacy_devotion_miracle.htm> accessed 16 March 2015.

Four years later he wrote,

> The diocese and Cathedral are dedicated to Our Lady of
> Perpetual Succour. Great undoubtedly are the graces which
> have been given during and since the Mission. Indeed, I
> may say, a special blessing seems to have descended on
> Middlesbrough since the church was dedicated to her, and
> more particularly since the picture was exposed in the Lady
> chapel. Some of the most abandoned and inveterate sinners
> have had the grace of conversion, and some have changed
> into saints. The tone of Catholicity is much improved in
> the town; the Faith of the people has completely revived;
> indeed it is as strong here as it is in Ireland itself.[10]

Bishop Lacy's healing at the shrine of Our Mother of Perpetual Succour

Bishop Lacy acknowledged great spiritual miracles that happened
through devotion to Our Lady of Perpetual Succour. On 21 March
1884 he wrote to tell a Redemptorist friend about his own physical
healing through the intercession of Our Blessed Lady. His letter is
worth quoting in full:

> My dear Fr Livius,
> After having sent off to the printer my little preface, as I
> informed you in my last letter, my next step was to go on
> the 18th to the Shrine of Our Lady of Perpetual Succour
> on the Esquiline[11] and offer up the Holy Sacrifice for a
> very special intention. Our Lady heard my prayer and
> vouchsafed me a miraculous cure of an internal ailment
> which has for the last nine years caused me much trouble
> and suffering, and has been a sad drawback to me in my
> work. The cure was instantaneous and complete.

10 John Coyle C.Ss.R., *Our Lady of Perpetual Succour and Ireland* (Dublin: Gill & Co., 1913), p. 161.
11 The church of St Alphonsus with Our Lady's shrine is built on the Esquiline hill in Rome.

At first I could hardly believe it. I felt confused at the thought of a miracle being wrought on me. It has, however, proved not to be imagination but reality. I need not say how overwhelmed I felt with a sense of gratitude for such a favour. For the honour of Our Lady of Perpetual Succour I think this ought to be made known, although if I were guided by my own natural instincts, I should prefer my name not to appear. I wish you would get as many prayers of thanksgiving as possible for this extraordinary proof of our Lady's loving heart. The good Fathers at St Alphonsus are all delighted and especially Fr Douglas. Believe me, my dear Father.

Yours faithfully in Christ

Richard, Bishop of Middlesbrough[12]

The devotion spreads worldwide

Devotion to Our Lady Perpetual Succour spread very rapidly throughout the Church. In the words of the American Redemptorist Fr Raymond Spitzer,

> Ireland can claim the glory for forming the first Confraternity of Our Mother of Perpetual Help. In 1868, two years after the picture had been enshrined in St Alphonsus' church in Rome, the people of Limerick organised their powerful sodality to spread devotion to our Lady of Perpetual Help throughout the length and breadth of the Isle of Saints. The following year witnessed the founding of a confraternity in Roulers, Belgium; the organization was sponsored by the hierarchy of that country, and within a year's time numbered 6400 members. Because of these and similar attempts to organize leagues of prayer to Our Lady, the most Reverend Father Nicholas

---

12 Ferreira, *Bishop Lacy.*

Mauron, the Superior General of the Redemptorists, petitioned the Holy Father, Pope Pius IX, that a pious confraternity in honour of Our Mother of Perpetual Help, and under the protection of St Alphonsus Maria de' Liguori might be established according to the laws of the Church at the church of St Alphonsus on the Esquiline. The request was granted on May 23, 1871.[13]

As devotion to Our Mother of Perpetual Succour continued to spread very rapidly, confraternities and sodalities for the promotion of the devotion sprang up in many countries. In 1876 Fr Mauron approached Blessed Pius IX with another request. He asked that the Confraternity of Our Mother of Perpetual Succour at St Alphonsus' church be raised into an arch-confraternity so that all the confraternities throughout the world could share in the spiritual privileges that the Church had bestowed on St Alphonsus' confraternity. Blessed Pius IX not only agreed but asked that he should be inscribed as the first member of the new arch-confraternity. So the arch-confraternity of Our Lady of Perpetual Succour had as its very first member Blessed Pius IX. Pius IX was renowned for his great devotion to Our Blessed Lady. He had proclaimed the dogma of Our Lady's Immaculate Conception in 1854.

Leo XIII, who succeeded Blessed Pius IX, kept a picture of Our Mother of Perpetual Succour on his desk, where he could see it throughout the day. His successor, St Pius X, granted an indulgence to anyone who prayed, "Mother of Perpetual Succour, pray for us". Benedict XV had a picture of Our Mother of Perpetual Succour placed immediately over the chair of state in the throne room where he received dignitaries from around the world. With the encouragement and example of these great popes, devotion to Our Mother of Perpetual Succour was fostered by the Redemptorists wherever they found themselves. New shrines to Our Lady were being erected, new novenas were being promoted, and thousands

13   R.J. Spitzer C.Ss.R., *The Miraculous Image of Our Mother of Perpetual Help* (Liguori, 1954), p. 53.

of copies and prints of the famous icon were being sent all over the world. It was truly the "Icon of Love", loved and reverenced by Catholics all over the world from the moment they first set their eyes on it. The beauty of the icon captivated their hearts. It spoke its profound message to them.

During the three hundred years that the miraculous icon attracted the veneration of the faithful who prayed at the shrine in the old St Matthew's, and where many miracles, both spiritual and physical, were experienced, there is no record of the devotion spreading beyond Rome. The same can be said of those years when the icon was on the island of Crete; devotion to Our Mother of Perpetual Succour did not spread beyond the island. But from the very first day that the miraculous icon arrived at the Redemptorist church of St Alphonsus, devotion to Our Lady of Perpetual Succour began to spread throughout the world. As we saw above, even within a month of the icon finding its new home in St Alphonsus' church in Rome, the Redemptorists in Liverpool were making a novena for the healing of Fr Hall.

Fr John Coyle C.Ss.R., writing in 1913, said, "Less than fifty years ago the Picture was hidden and unknown, today it is known and reverenced and loved in all Lands, even to the very ends of the earth." And he quotes the reading from the first Divine Office of Our Lady of Perpetual Succour:

> Since the time that the holy Picture was, by the special Providence of God, recovered from oblivion and restored once more to public veneration, it has been famous for such numerous and striking miracles and marvels of grace, that within the space of only a few years the devotion to the Madonna of Perpetual Succour has spread throughout the entire Christian world.[14]

---

14 Coyle, *Our Lady of Perpetual Succour and Ireland*, p. 145.

The amazing spread of devotion, with the revival of faith and trust that accompanied it, was in itself miraculous. The fountain of grace was flowing copiously. But how could the pastors of the Church, especially the Redemptorist missionaries, channel and foster this great current of grace? In many parts of the world devotion to Our Lady of Perpetual Succour began to take the form of the Perpetual Novena. We will look briefly at this extraordinary development in the next chapter.

— Chapter 3 —

The Perpetual Novena to Our Lady of Perpetual Succour

The fountain of grace that opened for the whole Church in 1866, when the miraculous Icon of Our Lady of Perpetual Succour was enshrined in the church of St Alphonsus in Rome, has touched and revived the hearts of millions all over the world, through the religious exercise that has been called the "Perpetual Novena". Wise pastoral leaders realised that the immense devotional enthusiasm aroused in multitudes of men and women as they venerated the mother of Jesus with expectant faith needed to be carefully channelled within the Catholic community. It was not just an individualistic devotion. It was a community devotion. The community, therefore, had a responsibility to find ways both to keep the spark of the devotion aglow and at the same time to help the devotees to deepen their understanding of their Christian faith and of Mary's role in their lives as the Mother of the Church. The form that the devotion began to take was that of the "Perpetual Novena". This is a weekly service of prayer consisting of: set prayers and hymns to Our Lady; a reading from scripture; a short homily; a reading of a selection of written petitions for Our Lady's help and thanksgivings for answers to prayer received; and the Benediction of the Blessed Sacrament. The whole service normally takes no longer than thirty minutes. After the service there is always the opportunity to celebrate the sacrament of reconciliation.

In his three-volume study, *Holy Mary of Perpetual Help*, Adelino Garcia Paz lists seventy countries in which the Perpetual Novena to Our Lady of Perpetual Succour continues to be a source of great spiritual renewal. This worldwide spread of the Perpetual Novena to Our Lady of Perpetual Succour is in itself an extraordinary sign of the power of this devotion. Fifty years ago an old parish priest explained to me very simply the attraction of the Perpetual Novena. "People", he said, "will come out to pray for their family, their loved ones and themselves when they get the opportunity. And the weekly novena provides them with a heaven-sent opportunity." People experienced the help, the "perpetual succour" that Our Lady offers to those who come to her. That is why Redemptorist missionaries, who had first-hand experience of the tremendous blessings that devotion to Our Mother of Perpetual Succour brings to people, began to introduce the pastoral practice of the Perpetual Novena in the parishes or cities that invited them to preach parish missions.

The Perpetual Novena to Our Lady of Perpetual Succour takes place each week. People can join the novena any week and continue to pray for their loved ones and themselves. A prayer petition box is placed before the shrine of Our Lady. This encourages people to write out their petitions, asking Our Lady for her help with some situation or giving thanks for graces already received. The reading out of some of these petitions during the service, so often expressed with great simplicity, faith and confidence, creates a wonderfully expectant atmosphere in the church. People are bringing all their family needs and their own personal needs to their mother. There is no human need, too enormous and seemingly "hopeless" or too small and apparently of little real consequence, that we should not bring to Our Mother of Perpetual Succour. It is a real spiritual tonic to hear the faith of people, often expressed in very simple and childlike words, as they ask their heavenly mother for help. They believe with their whole heart that Mary hears and answers our prayers. She never refuses to listen to our petitions. She is there to help even before we have the confidence to ask. That is why she herself named the miraculous icon "Our Lady of Perpetual Succour". The word "succour" comes from the Latin word *succurrere*, which literally means "to run under". That is what a mother does when she sees her child in danger. She runs to help; she runs to get beneath the danger and protect her child. So, although in some countries, especially in the USA, people can rightly refer to the icon as Our Lady of Perpetual Help, in Britain we still prefer to speak of Our Lady of Perpetual Succour. The word "succour" gives us a richer and more comprehensive meaning of the all-embracing help that Our Lady offers.

Hearing these petitions read out gives great witness to the trust that the petitioners are placing in Our Lady. They are sharing their faith with the community on a very deep and personal level and that renews the faith of the community. But the petitioners, in their turn, become the thanksgivers. Inspiring "thank you" notes to Our Lady for favours received are also read out. The novena service becomes a great public witness to the people's faith in God who answers prayers through the intercession of Our Lady. In an age of doubt and scepticism, that witness is more than ever necessary for our Catholic communities.

The prayer of faith

The graces received, for which people are giving thanks, are granted through the prayer of the community. The novena has the power to engage and activate the "prayer of faith" of the community assembled to honour Our Mother of Perpetual Succour. In the liturgy of the sacrament of the anointing of the sick we are told that:

> The community, asking God's help for the sick, makes its prayer of faith in response to God's word and in a spirit of trust (see James 5:14-15). In the rites for the sick, it is the people of God who pray in faith.[1]

In a similar way, it is the community gathered in the name of Jesus to honour Our Mother of Perpetual Succour that says the "prayer

---

1   Anointing of the Sick, 105.

of faith" as they bring all their needs, especially the needs of those who are sick or finding life burdensome, to their heavenly mother. Jesus himself promises,

> I tell you solemnly once again, if two of you on earth agree to ask anything at all, it will be granted to you by my Father in heaven. For where two or three meet in my name, I shall be there with them (Matthew 18:19-20).

The novena engages this faith in Jesus' presence in our midst as we gather in his name to honour our heavenly mother who is, of course, his mother too.

Origin of the Perpetual Novena

The first weekly novena to Our Mother of Perpetual Succour began in the Redemptorist church in St Louis, USA, in 1922. A large crowd gathered each Tuesday to venerate Our Lady and bring all their petitions to her. In 1926, to accommodate the increasing numbers of people wanting to "make the novena", a second service was held each Tuesday. In 1928 the novena was called "the Perpetual Novena". By March 1930 the numbers wishing to make the novena were so large that six sessions a day were introduced. In June of that year there were seven daily sessions. And by December of the same year there were ten daily sessions with 7,500 people faithfully making the novena each Tuesday. This was a whole new experience of the power of devotion to Our Lady of Perpetual Succour. This form of the Perpetual Novena spread so rapidly throughout the USA that in the 1960s the Perpetual Novena to Our Mother of Perpetual Succour was being held in around two thousand parish churches. It had become a religious phenomenon.

From the United States it spread to other English-speaking countries, often through the advocacy of the American Redemptorist army chaplains who were stationed with American soldiers in different parts of the world during the Second World War. Two of these chaplains introduced the practice of the Perpetual Novena to Clonard, the Redemptorist monastery church in Belfast, in 1943. From there it spread throughout Ireland and to Britain. In the 1960s some two hundred parish churches in Britain had the Perpetual Novena each week. Very soon the Perpetual Novena devotions spread throughout the world. Wherever Redemptorists preached parish missions they would establish the "Perpetual Novena" as the great means for keeping the faith and the devotion of the people alive. Also, many parish priests who were brought up on devotion to Our Lady of Perpetual Succour wanted to introduce the novena to their parishes. In the 1960s the Perpetual Novena to Our Lady of Perpetual Succour was celebrated each week in thousands of parishes around the Catholic world.

Blessed Paul VI

On 25 March 1966, as the Redemptorists were preparing to celebrate the hundredth anniversary of the restoration of the miraculous icon to public veneration in the church of St Alphonsus in Rome, Blessed Paul VI wrote to their Superior General acknowledging the part that Redemptorist missionaries had played in fostering this devotion to Our Lady. He wrote:

> You, Redemptorists, are entitled to the honour of having restored the devotion to Our Lady of Perpetual Succour and of having diffused it throughout the world. You yourselves have shown her a very great devotion. You have observed faithfully the recommendation of our predecessor to spread devotion to the Virgin of Perpetual Succour throughout the world. Today the veneration of Perpetual Succour is found in every nation, thanks above all to your efforts and interest. This anniversary is a new motive for you to increase more and more your devotion to Mary of Perpetual Succour.[2]

---

2   Adelino M Garcia Paz, *Holy Mary of Perpetual Help*, vol. III: *Person and Practices* (Singapore: Redemptorist Community, 1991), p. 26.

41

Blessed Paul VI was fully aware of the extraordinary numbers of the faithful who were making the novena around the world in 1966. Fifty years later, in our own time, as we will see, in some countries there has been a marked decline in the numbers attending the novena, and indeed in the number of churches that have the novena. Yet in many countries the devotion to Our Lady of Perpetual Succour is still vibrant. In some cities the numbers attending the weekly novena are truly phenomenal. We will mention just a few.

Manila

The Redemptorist church in Baclaran, Manila, has been officially declared the national sanctuary of the Mother of Perpetual Succour by the Catholic bishops of the Philippines. Every Wednesday around 100,000 people attend the novena services. There are five Masses and ten sessions during the day in a church that can seat two thousand, with room for another nine thousand standing. I had heard about these phenomenal numbers for years, but it was only when I had the opportunity to be present at the sessions, when I was giving a retreat to priests in the Philippines, that I realised what an extraordinary source of grace the novena is for so many people. All day long thousands of men and women filled the church for each session and at each session they filled the church with their faith and devotion. During the priests' retreat I encountered the same wonderful devotion to Our Lady. These priests had that same total confidence in Our Mother of Perpetual Succour.

Our Lady's sanctuary at Baclaran was well known to St John Paul II. When he began his apostolic journey to Asia in February 1981 he went straight from the airport in Manila to the shrine in Baclaran. In the midst of a congregation of many thousands he prayed:

> Oh Mother of Perpetual Succour. I am able to come here for the second time. The first time I stopped here on my way to the Eucharistic Congress in Australia. Then, when I

was at Mass in the evening, I was witness to the truly filial devotion that you enjoy among the faithful, and the people, who live in this great capital city of the Philippines... At the beginning of the pastoral visit in the Far East I recommend to you and into your hands with total confidence, all the nations and peoples of Asia and its islands located nearby. Mother of Perpetual Succour, accept this humble offering and place it in the heart of your Son, remembering that when you were near the Cross on Calvary, every one of us was entrusted to you as to our Mother, Amen.[3]

The grace that flows from their great devotion to Our Lady of Perpetual Succour keeps the faith of millions in the Philippines alive and active. Pope Francis celebrated his final Mass during his visit to the Philippines on 18 January 2015 with a congregation of six million, the biggest Mass congregation in history.

Singapore

In the Redemptorist parish of St Alphonsus in Singapore each Saturday there are ten sessions of the novena. The novena is such a notable public event in that great city that, when the metro system was being built in 1987, the station next to the church was called "Novena". A special feature of this novena is the presence of many non-Christians, Buddhists and devotees of Hinduism. Very often when the letters of thanksgiving to Our Lady for favours received are read out, the non-Christian participants are thanking their Christian friends who brought them to the novena and introduced them to Our Lady of Perpetual Succour. Many of them become Christians. While I was giving a priests' retreat in Singapore I had the opportunity to give a weekend retreat to 150 lay charismatic leaders. Many of them said to me that their first contact with Christianity was the novena. And they would add, "It was the Mother that brought me to Jesus." One parish priest was able to say that of the 290 baptisms he

---

3   Adelino M. Garcia Paz, *Holy Mary of Perpetual Help*, vol. II: *Geography and Significance of the Devotion* (Singapore: Redemptorist Community, 1991), p. 152.

administered in his parish in one year, ninety per cent of the newly baptised felt their first attraction to the faith through the novena.

The Perpetual Novena has an amazing evangelising effect on the non-Christian participants. Only three per cent of the inhabitants of Singapore are Catholic; twenty-five per cent of the 15,000 weekly attendance at the novena services in the church of St Alphonsus are non-Christian. By "making Our Lady of Perpetual Succour known" in Singapore the Redemptorists have found a most effective method of evangelisation.

India

The Irish Redemptorists began their mission foundations in India in 1939. They brought with them devotion to Our Mother of Perpetual Succour and introduced the Perpetual Novena in Mumbai (Bombay) in 1948. The response of the citizens of that great city was phenomenal:

> About 40,000 participate on Wednesday in the exercise of the Novena, repeated twelve times a day in order to be able to accommodate the devotees. 80 per cent of the participants are non-Catholic. This is something very striking; there are Hindus, Parsis, Muslims etc. The prayers are recited in different languages: English, Marathi and Konkani.[4]

Canada

The Redemptorists introduced devotion to Our Mother of Perpetual Succour as soon as they arrived at St Patrick's church in McCaul Street in Toronto. The devotion spread rapidly all over Canada. Today, despite all the social changes that have affected that great city, the Perpetual Novena still attracts each Wednesday 2,000 to 2,500 men and women who come to honour their heavenly mother and to implore her help in all their needs. Each Wednesday there

---

4   Garcia Paz, *Holy Mary of Perpetual Help*, vol. II, p. 159.

are six Masses to accommodate the numbers wishing to make the novena. The first Mass begins at 7.30 a.m. and the last Mass begins at 7.00 p.m. There is an average attendance of 350 to 400 people at each Mass. The sacrament of reconciliation is available for half an hour before each Mass. This is a continuous mission at the heart of a great city. It has been referred to as "the miracle of McCaul Street". The Wednesday novena, with large crowds making their way to the church of St Patrick six times during the day, gives a powerful, public witness to Christian faith at the heart of a great city.

Poland

The National Marian shrine of Our Lady of Czestochowa, known as the Black Madonna, is the third largest Catholic pilgrimage site in the world. It is the centre of Polish Catholicism. Polish Catholics have been renowned for their fervent devotion to Our Lady of Czestochowa. But they also enthusiastically embraced devotion to Our Mother of Perpetual Succour. The Redemptorists were expelled from Poland by the Government of the time in the early nineteenth century. They were allowed to return in 1893. Fr Bernard Lubienski, the son of an aristocratic family, became a Redemptorist while studying in England. He made his novitiate year in Bishop Eton, the Redemptorist community in Liverpool, where he was professed in May 1866, just a month after the miraculous icon of Our Mother of Perpetual Succour was enshrined in St Alphonsus' church in Rome. He was a novice in the community when Fr Hall was miraculously cured and the chronicler wrote, "Today the house of Bishop Eton was filled with joy and gratitude at the miraculous cure of Rev. Fr Hall, through the intercession of the Madonna of Perpetual Succour."[5]

Fr Lubienski had, therefore, first-hand experience of the healing power of devotion to Our Mother of Perpetual Succour. He was ordained a priest in 1870. After twenty years of missionary work in England and Scotland he was providentially able to reintroduce the

---

5   William Raemers C.Ss.R., *The Mother of Perpetual Succour* (London: Catholic Truth Society, 1939), p. 17.

Redemptorists to his homeland in Poland in 1893. He introduced the people of Poland to Our Mother of Perpetual Succour. His missionary work was greatly blessed. Many young Polish men became Redemptorists. Devotion to Our Lady of Perpetual Succour spread so quickly throughout Poland that Adelino Garcia Paz can write, "The Perpetual Novena began on 23 January 1951 and was held in nearly 2,000 churches."[6] A phenomenal manifestation of the Marian piety of the Polish people!

St John Paul II, in the year of his golden jubilee of priesthood, reflected on the beginnings of his vocation:

> In speaking of the origin of my priestly vocation, I cannot overlook its Marian thread. I learned the traditional devotions to the Mother of God in my family and in my parish in Wadowice. I remember, in the parish church, a side chapel dedicated to Our Lady of Perpetual Succour. In the mornings, the secondary school students would make a visit to it before classes began. After classes, in the afternoon, many students would go there to pray to the Blessed Virgin.[7]

And, as a young man during the Nazi occupation of his country, he would visit the Redemptorist church in Kraków on his way home from work. During a visit to the shrine of Our Mother of Perpetual Succour in the church of St Alphonsus in 1991, St John Paul II spoke about those visits to the shrine in the Redemptorist church in Kraków during the war:

> I remember that during World War II, during the time of the Nazi occupation of Poland, I was a factory worker in Kraków. On my way home, after work, since it was on my way, I always stopped at the Redemptorist church. In the church there was the picture of Perpetual Succour. I used to stop there, not only because it was on my way back,

---

6   Garcia Paz, *Holy Mary of Perpetual Help*, vol. II, p. 68.
7   St John Paul II, *Gift and Mystery* (London: Catholic Truth Society, 1997), p. 27.

but because that picture just seemed so beautiful. And I kept visiting that church even after I was named bishop and cardinal.[8]

As a young schoolboy in Wadowice and as a young man, labouring in Nazi-occupied Kraków, Karol Wojtyla, the future pope and great saint, St John Paul II, found peace and tranquillity kneeling before the image of Our Mother of Perpetual Succour. For him it was the Icon of Love. In his own words, it "just seemed so beautiful".

Britain

In Britain the Perpetual Novena to Our Mother of Perpetual Succour began in the 1940s and reached its peak in the 1970s and into the 1980s, the decades after the Second Vatican Council. The Redemptorists in Britain published a monthly magazine with the title *The Novena* to promote the devotion to Our Mother of Perpetual Succour. The magazine had a wide circulation in the parishes of England and Scotland, especially in the parishes where the Perpetual Novena took place. Around two hundred churches had the weekly novena. Redemptorist Fr Michael Creech describes his own memory of the Perpetual Novena being introduced in the Redemptorist parish of St Mary, Clapham Common, in London, where he was an altar server at the time:

> It was in the mid-forties as the Second World War was grinding to a halt, that we saw a number of American military chaplains pass through Clapham. They were popular with the altar servers for their warm, cheerful dispositions, as well as the occasional dollar they would donate to the poor children of London. The scars of war on the home front were everywhere.
>
> We did not know what conversations were taking place in the monastery between the Redemptorist community and

---

8 *Our Lady of Perpetual Help: The Icon, Favours and Shrines* (Rome: Church of St Alphonsus, 1997), p. 35.

the visiting Redemptorist military chaplains, but suddenly the launching of a Perpetual Novena in honour of Our Lady of Perpetual Succour was announced. This was something new. We were familiar with Wednesday evening devotions in honour of St Joseph and devotions to the Holy Infant on the 25th of each month – not forgetting the "Rosary, sermon and benediction" every Sunday night.

As far as I can remember an American chaplain conducted the first novena service, with the resident community watching on. We were intrigued, as servers, with the introduction of St Alphonsus' prayer during the exposition of the Blessed Sacrament, as well as the procession to the Lady chapel for the final hymn. It was full of stories of how people were being blessed, all over the world, with great answers to their prayers at the novena.[9]

The Perpetual Novena appealed to many parish priests who wanted to introduce the weekly devotion to their people. The icon of Our Lady of Perpetual Succour found a place of honour in many churches in England, Scotland and Wales. Three of the English dioceses, Middlesbrough, Leeds and Hallam, have Our Mother of Perpetual Succour as their patroness.

Since the late 1970s there has been a great decline in the numbers making the weekly novena in many churches. Cultural changes in many societies deter people from making weekly commitments. The generation that was "brought up on novenas" and similar devotions to Mary is no longer with us. But Our Mother of Perpetual Succour remains with us. Devotion to Our Lady of Perpetual Succour has flowed through the Church, bringing spiritual, mental and physical health and strength to many millions. As we approach the 150th anniversary, each of us is invited to renew our devotion and open our hearts in new ways to Our Mother of Perpetual Succour. She

---

9   Personal note to author.

knows our hearts, answers our prayers, and obtains for each of us the renewal of our faith and trust in Jesus our saviour when we most need it. Her help is constant and that is why we call it "perpetual". It never ceases.

The Solemn Novena to Our Mother of Perpetual Succour

Devotion to Our Mother of Perpetual Succour has revived in new forms in the past twenty or thirty years. In many places in Britain and Ireland parishes have "the nine days' prayer" or the "Solemn Novena" in honour of Our Mother of Perpetual Succour. The annual Solemn Novena, in preparation for the celebration of the liturgical feast of Our Mother of Perpetual Succour on 27 June, has become a major manifestation of faith in many parts of the world. In the Redemptorist church of St Mary in Clapham Common, London, where I am based, I am always deeply impressed by the large numbers who travel from different parts of the Greater London area to "make the novena". At each session some of the petitions that have been placed in the "petition box" in the shrine are read out. It is truly uplifting to hear the faith and confidence with which people bring all their needs, all their fears and trouble, to Our Lady. Then we hear the letters of thanksgiving from grateful petitioners who have had their prayers answered. As we listen to both the petitions for help and the thanksgivings for help received, we get a real sense of Our Lady's motherly presence with and care for her children. When a congregation is united in their love of Our Lady and ask with confidence for her maternal help, miracles do happen: depression is lifted, fears are banished, hope is restored, heart and soul are filled with joy, and people walk out of the church feeling well again and ready to face their future with renewed courage and hope. All these answers to prayer are experienced as miracles. And those who experience them acknowledge them in the thanksgiving notes that they put in the petition box at the shrine of Our Lady of Perpetual Succour.

At the Solemn Novena in June 2014 a mother received a very big blessing and answer to her prayer for her son. When he was sixteen he suffered some kind of major trauma that made him retreat into himself and he became silent. For ten years he maintained his silence in the home, never communicating, but never aggressive in any way. During the healing prayer his mother poured out her heart to Our Mother of Perpetual Succour. When she returned home that evening her son began to speak to her. The following evening he came to the novena. Since then he has got a job and is continuing to make great progress.

The experience of the Solemn Novena in St Mary's in Clapham Common is repeated in our Redemptorist churches in Birmingham and Liverpool. Thousands of men and women make the Solemn Novena each year because they have experienced the power of God working in their lives as they gather to honour Our Mother of Perpetual Succour. In other churches throughout England and Scotland where Our Mother of Perpetual Succour is honoured, people continue to receive great blessings. The fountain of grace continues to overflow, refreshing all who open their hearts to Our Lady.

Ireland

In Ireland, the Solemn Novena attracts tens of thousands of the faithful. In Limerick city, where the first confraternity of Our Mother of Perpetual Succour was established in 1868, just two years after the miraculous icon was enshrined in the church of St Alphonsus in Rome, the Solemn Novena at Mount St Alphonsus church draws very large crowds each year. In 2014, 10,000 men and women attended the novena services. There are ten services throughout the day, beginning at 7.30 a.m. and concluding with the night service at 10.30 p.m. It is a day-long celebration of faith and hope and a sure sign that despite all the difficulties and hardships that the Church in Ireland has experienced in recent decades, the faithful's love for and trust in Our Mother of Perpetual Succour remains undiminished. Similar large crowds make the Solemn Novena to Our Mother of Perpetual Succour in Belfast, at the Redemptorists' Clonard Monastery church. In 2012 the BBC Northern Ireland news announced the start of the novena with these words: "The Catholic church on Belfast's Falls Road draws pilgrims from across Northern Ireland every June. The annual Festival of Faith is rooted in Catholic devotion to the Virgin Mary and nine successive days of services known as a novena. About 15,000 people are expected to attend the sessions at Clonard Monastery in West Belfast." The Solemn Novena in Clonard is often referred to as the Belfast miracle. Many Protestant Christians attend the services, and Protestant minsters lead some services. When Fr Tim Buckley C.Ss.R., a Londoner, preached at the Clonard novena I asked him to describe his experience. He wrote as follows:

> From Wednesday June 17 to Thursday June 25 1998 I was privileged to be one of the team of preachers for the Solemn Novena in honour of Our Lady of Perpetual Succour at Clonard Monastery in Belfast. While I had heard many accounts of the extraordinary nature of this annual event, which attracts crowds of over 15,000 each day, nothing could have prepared me for the quite overwhelmingly moving experience of the event itself. The vast majority of those who take part are Roman Catholics, but it was heartening to see that people of all ages and from across the political and religious divide attend. They pack the church, surrounding monastery corridors and garden for the ten sessions, beginning at 7.30 in the morning and ending in candlelight just before midnight. In an extraordinary operation with back-up teams of priests and people, ministering the Eucharist and available for counselling and the Sacrament of Reconciliation, supported by an army of volunteers stewarding each session.

As the Novena unfolded I tried to identify the key factors which were having such an enormous effect on me. Two emerged strongly. Firstly I was touched by the fact that the prayer of faith of this community was expressed in such a down-to-earth and practical way. The preaching was direct and immediate: it touched into the lives of a people who have suffered so much in recent years, but whose hope seemed almost tangible. Their response was to pour out their prayers in petitions that sometimes reminded me of the openness and forthrightness of the Old Testament prophets and psalmists, pleading with God to be with them and to save them.

Secondly I was struck that once again it was Mary who was the catalyst for this remarkable demonstration of faith. I say "once again" because the only comparable experience I could think of was that of Lourdes. There too Mary is the cause of thousands of people gathering to present to God their prayers for healing and strength. In this secular society these shrines and centres of devotion provide havens where it is the done thing for people to be seen praying and celebrating their faith, and where the social order is *supplanted* by the gospel order. By contrast, here the poor, the sick, the handicapped, those in distress of any kind take centre stage: here we can get a glimpse of what Jesus means when he teaches us the *beatitudes* and tells us that *the last shall be first.*

I experienced during the days of the novena a profound sense of what it means to be part of the family of faith, united in prayer with one another, as well as with those who have gone before us – the communion of saints in heaven – and above all with Mary, the mother of the family.[10]

---

[10] Fr Tim Buckley's eloquent account of his experience was written for and published in Jim McManus, *All Generations Will Call Me Blessed: Mary at the Millennium* (Chawton: Redemptorist Publications, 2007).

Hundreds of thousands of people around the Catholic world will attend such Solemn Novenas, the kind that Fr Tim Buckley described above. There is a pastoral lesson in this for the Church. As well as beautiful liturgy during the celebration of Mass people yearn for devotional exercises that fill them with hope and confidence in the powerful intercession of Our Lady. Catholics welcome the opportunity to pray for the needs of their families and their personal needs; they need the support of the community of faith in bringing their needs confidently to God; they need to experience the atmosphere of faith and expectation that a good spiritual event creates. A nine days' prayer event provides them with that opportunity – it is not a long-term commitment but, at the same time, it is long enough to give people the religious sense that they are involved in real community prayer and spiritual renewal. As we celebrate the 150th anniversary of the gift of the Icon of Love, the beautiful picture of Our Mother of Perpetual Succour, to the pastoral care of the Redemptorists in Rome, and as we recall all the grace that devotion to Our Lady has brought to millions of men and women in the past 150 years, we want to pray for a renewal of this devotion in our own hearts and throughout the Church. The simple prayer, "Mother of Perpetual Succour, pray for us", will always be heard in heaven.

— Chapter 4 —

The Home Novena to Our Mother of Perpetual Succour

The history of 150 years of public devotion to Our Mother of Perpetual Succour shows us clearly that this devotion has truly been a fountain of grace for millions of Catholics and, indeed, many thousands of non-Catholic and non-Christian devotees of Our Lady. They have felt blessed and nourished, supported and encouraged, healed and comforted by participating in the Perpetual Novena to Our Mother of Perpetual Succour. They knew that they could bring all their joys and all their sorrows to Our Lady and experience her maternal succour in their every need. They not only presented their requests in the petition box before the shrine, but they also wrote beautiful notes of thanks for favours received, which were read out and inspired even greater confidence in all those attending the novena. The novena has provided a grace-filled, faith-sharing experience for millions.

Make her known to the whole world

Blessed Pius IX, when he entrusted to the Redemptorists the miraculous icon of Our Mother of Perpetual Succour in 1866, exhorted them, as we have seen, "to make her known to the whole world". In response to the Pope's exhortation and out of love for Our Lady, Redemptorist missionaries made it their special pastoral responsibility to promote this devotion to Our Mother of Perpetual Succour. Wherever possible, they introduced the Perpetual Novena in parishes all over the world; and many other parishes, on their own initiative, seeing the fruits of the devotion, took up the practice of the weekly novena. As we saw in the previous chapter, the novena flourished all over the world in tens of thousands of parishes. In many parishes today, however, these weekly devotions to Our Lady no longer take place.

When viewed in the light of the extraordinary graces that so many people received by their weekly participation in those devotions, this decline can be difficult to understand. Why did this happen? Did people no longer have the opportunity to attend a novena service in their local church? Or was devotion so "privatised" that parishioners no longer felt the need to cultivate their devotion to the Mother of God as a community? Or did the Sunday Mass answer all the needs of the human heart for true devotion? No doubt there are many reasons that can be put forward to explain the decline in the attendance at the weekly novenas. This is not the place to attempt a sociological analysis of why this decline has happened.

We still need to drink from the fountain of grace

My purpose in writing this book is to refocus our attention on this fountain of grace that is devotion to Our Mother of Perpetual Succour. We still need to drink from this fountain. The Catholic soul needs to be nourished on a true devotion to the mother of Jesus because, in God's plan for our salvation, she has become our mother too. Writing on the occasion of the centenary of the miraculous icon being enshrined for public veneration in the church of St Alphonsus, Blessed Paul VI said:

> The very expressive title of Perpetual Succour with which the Virgin is invoked summarises the teaching of the Second Vatican Council about Mary, Mother of the Church, and urges the faithful to have confidence in her. Mary was the succour of the Church when she gave us Christ and when she accompanied him in the work of Redemption. She continues to be our succour now, after her Assumption body and soul into heaven.[1]

---

1   Adelino M. Garcia Paz, *Holy Mary of Perpetual Help*, vol. III: *Person and Practices* (Singapore: Redemptorist Community, 1991), p. 26.

Although forms of our devotion to Our Lady change from age to age, devotion itself remains a vital part of Catholic life and spirituality. In our time we have to ensure that true devotion to Our Lady is preserved in our Catholic communities and handed on to future generations.

New missionaries

For the changing times we need new missionary perspectives and new missionaries. Pope Francis has identified the new missionaries:

> In virtue of their baptism, all the members of the People of God have become missionary disciples (cf. Matthew 28:19). All the baptized, whatever their position in the Church or their level of instruction in the faith, are agents of evangelization, and it would be insufficient to envisage a plan of evangelization to be carried out by professionals while the rest of the faithful would simply be passive recipients. The new evangelization calls for personal involvement on the part of each of the baptized... we no longer say that we are "disciples" and "missionaries", but rather that we are always "missionary disciples".[2]

You are a "missionary disciple" of the Lord. Each missionary disciple today is being urged by Pope Francis to bring the Gospel to others. Bringing the good news of Christ to others will always mean introducing others to the mother of Jesus who is, by the gift and will of Jesus, their spiritual mother. The Church needs many "missionary disciples" today. The encouraging news is that those missionary disciples are rallying to the call.

New missionary perspectives

A true devotion to Our Mother of Perpetual Succour, while it is certainly greatly nourished by participation in a weekly parish

---

2   Pope Francis, *Evangelii Gaudium* ("The Joy of the Gospel"), 120.

celebration, can also be cultivated in the privacy of one's home and shared with the members of one's family or with a few friends. If you have never had the opportunity to attend a novena service you can still develop your devotion to Our Mother of Perpetual Succour privately. Indeed, you might even invite a few friends to join you in your home and say together the prayers of the novena for the needs of your family, your loved ones and the whole world.

Mothers' Prayer Movement

In recent years a new prayer movement has spread throughout the world. It is known as Mothers' Prayer Movement. Mothers and grandmothers, very aware of the pressures and dangers to which their children and grandchildren are exposed, be it drugs, internet pornography or violence, meet together in one another's homes or in some quiet place to pray for their children and grandchildren. This initiative was taken by Veronica Williams and her sister-in-law, both grandmothers, in 1995. In an interview with Zenit.org, a Catholic internet news agency, Veronica explained how and why she started this movement. She had been collaborating with a group of Christians in Kent who were preparing a report for the UK Parliament on what was happening to young people in our society. The title of the report was "What on earth are we doing to our children?" It was, as she said, full of statistics about drug abuse and other abuses and dangers. But she was very disappointed with the response from Parliament. She said,

> At the time I had nine grandchildren. I was so shocked when I read the report and I thought, what kind of society are my grandchildren growing up in? I wanted to do something but felt very small against such big problems. But I had just had a wonderful experience which made me understand the power of prayer, and of "surrendering everything to the Lord"…

I decided that I would pray for children, and my sister-in-law, who knew nothing about my decision to pray, told me that she was woken up during the night and felt a call to pray for her children… during one month we prayed and meditated on the third joyful mystery of the Rosary (Nativity of the Child Jesus) to ask him what he wanted us to do… And in November 1995 we started with three other mothers praying for our children.[3]

That faith initiative that Veronica and her small group of mothers took in 1995, in the front room of her home in Kent, has now become a worldwide prayer movement with mothers and grandmothers meeting to pray for their children and grandchildren in a hundred countries worldwide. As Veronica said,

We now have groups all over the world, probably 85% are Catholic, but there are mothers from different denominations: Pentecostals, Baptists, Anglicans, and Orthodox… And also some from other religions – Muslims and Hindus, and even atheists who come and find God. God is breaking down barriers.[4]

She describes the spirituality of the groups in this way:

Our particular spirituality is based on giving everything to Jesus: we don't give advice to solve problems. We say: "I can't do it, Lord, but you can". This is the way we surrender totally to the Lord. I know he opens doors. Miracles do happen. Children are coming back to faith in God, getting married, coming off drugs, children that have been missing are coming back home. Mothers experience a deeper personal experience with Christ, and come deeper into their traditional faith. Some that have left the Church have come back again.[5]

---

3   Veronica Williams, "The 'Mothers' Prayers' All Over the World", 8 March 2012 <http://www.zenit.org/en/articles/the-mothers-prayers-all-over-the-world> accessed 18 March 2015.

4   Williams, "The 'Mothers' Prayers' All Over the World".

5   Williams, "The 'Mothers' Prayers' All Over the World". For a very clear and inspiring vision of surrendering to the Lord, see Veronica Williams, *The Joy of Surrender unto Him* (Solace Community, 2004). This little book explains the spirituality of Mothers' Prayers.

Veronica's list of the graces of Mothers' Prayers reads like a list of graces that would have been read out at the Perpetual Novena services in parishes all over the world for the last ninety years. God answers prayer. But Veronica's experience shows us, just as the millions who flocked to the Perpetual Novena showed us, that we need support, the support of the small, intimate group of friends in the front room of one's home, or of the larger parish community group in the church, to persevere confidently in our prayer.

Home-based Perpetual Novena to Our Mother of Perpetual Succour

The worldwide Mothers' Prayer Movement provides us with a very good model for renewing and deepening our own devotion to Our Mother of Perpetual Succour. If you are in a parish, town or city where there is no public devotion to Our Mother of Perpetual Succour you might consider asking one or two friends to join you in your home to pray the novena prayers for your families. We all recognise that families are under great stress today, not just economic stress but emotional and spiritual stress. Pope Francis keeps reminding the whole Church that the mission of the Church in our times is to heal the wounds that so often paralyse individuals and sap their spiritual energy. He spelled out very clearly his vision of the healing ministry of the Church when he said:

> I see clearly that the thing the church needs most today is the ability to heal wounds and to warm the hearts of the faithful; it needs nearness, proximity. I see the church as a field hospital after battle. It is useless to ask a seriously injured person if he has high cholesterol and about the level of his blood sugars! You have to heal his wounds. Then we can talk about everything else. Heal the wounds, heal the wounds... And you have to start from the ground up.[6]

---

6   Interview with Fr Antonio Spadaro, published in *America*, 30 September 2013.

In his homily on 5 February 2015 he returned very forthrightly to his awareness of the need for healing in the Church today. He said,

> … there are many wounded people waiting in the aisles of the church for a minister of Christ to heal them. This requires healing the wounded hearts, opening doors, freeing people, and saying that God is good, forgives all, is our Father, is tender and always waiting for us.

Any person, clerical or lay, applying for a job in Pope Francis' " field hospital" would have to be ready and willing to get involved in the healing of the wounded. This is the necessary and urgent pastoral response that all "missionary disciples" have to make today.

Bemoaning the times we live in, because of all the emotional stresses and moral and ethical confusion, achieves no change for the better. Prayer to Our Mother of Perpetual Succour, seeking her powerful intercession, changes everything. She is "the Mother of the afflicted, the health of the sick, and the refuge of sinners". There is no situation in which she is not willing to get involved. She loves each individual in the world as her own son or daughter. But she depends on us to introduce some of them to her. Perhaps you know people, old and young, who really need Our Lady's special care? How can you make the introduction?

Your home as the new shrine to Our Mother of Perpetual Succour

You might feel inspired by initiatives like that of Veronica Williams to begin a new form of the Perpetual Novena based not in a parish church but in your own home. Your home could become the new shrine of Our Mother of Perpetual Succour where you and some of your friends could meet to honour Our Lady and ask her powerful intercession for all the needs of your families, the Church and the world. You could pray the novena prayers with the total confidence that every problem and every situation can be surrendered to Christ and that, at the intercession of Our Mother of Perpetual Succour, your prayers will be heard. Your friends, particularly grandparents and parents, may be waiting for someone to take this prayer initiative because they want to bring their own children and grandchildren under the protection of Our Lady. The fact that you have read this book so far may mean that you have the grace to take this prayer initiative. Talk to Our Lady about this over the next few days. As a missionary disciple you too want to "make her known". With her help you will discern the best way for ensuring that those you know, your family and friends, can still come to drink at the fountain of grace and relax in the presence of the Icon of Love.

Taking the opportunity

New initiatives are often the results of ordinary conversations. If you are in the habit of sharing with a few friends your own worries about the times we live in, the challenges facing families today, the economic uncertainties and the social and political upheavals that threaten the peace of so many countries, you might conclude your conversation with words like, "I believe God alone can resolve all these problems. I think the best thing we can do is to pray for our families and our world." If the people you are sharing with agree, then you could ask them if they would be willing to set aside about twenty minutes a week, at a time that suits them, to meet together for a time of prayer. If one or two of them agree you will have your prayer partners for the Home Novena and you will be able to foster a true devotion to Our Mother of Perpetual Succour. All that is needed for great things to happen in the world of faith is for a few people to come together and pray.

The mustard-seed model

Jesus gives us this image of what the kingdom of God is like:

> The kingdom of heaven is like a mustard seed which a man took and sowed in his field. It is the smallest of all seeds,

> but when it has grown it is the biggest shrub of all and becomes a tree so that the birds of the air come and shelter in its branches (Matthew 13:31-32).

That is the Lord's own image of how we begin working for the kingdom of God. We don't look for big numbers or give up because just a few respond. The few are the mustard seed of the kingdom of God. Jesus reinforces the significance of the few gathered in his name when he says,

> I tell you solemnly once again, if two of you on earth agree to ask anything at all, it will be granted to you by my Father in heaven. For where two or three meet in my name, I shall be there with them (Matthew 18:19-20).

If you and a few of your friends come together to honour Our Mother of Perpetual Succour and to pray for your families and those in need, you will have planted the mustard seed. The Home Novena is the mustard seed of the kingdom of God.

Healing of the whole family

Devotion to Our Mother of Perpetual Succour continues to be a fountain of grace, a source of healing for the whole family. The very presence of the miraculous icon brings the presence of Our Lady into your home. The home that has a place for Our Lady will always experience her powerful protection and her healing presence.

The Home Novena, shared within the family and with a few friends, becomes the weekly manifestation of total trust in the protection of Our Mother of Perpetual Succour. She encourages us to come to her and lay all our cares and worries before her, because Jesus has given her to us to be our spiritual mother and she yearns to care for us. In our novena prayer we are not desperately trying to "catch her attention". Her eyes are focused on us all the time and she is waiting for us to turn to her in love and prayer. One look at the picture shows us that her eyes are on us.

You can have that consoling and comforting experience in your own living room or bedroom if you find a place for a copy of the miraculous icon. If you haven't got the icon of Our Mother of Perpetual Succour in your home you can download beautiful copies from the internet, free of charge. And you could share that consolation with your friends, who may be in need of some help, by giving them the opportunity to get to know Our Mother of Perpetual Succour in the Home Novena. In the Appendix of this book you will find the prayers of the novena.

The introduction

Sometimes people who have forgotten about the help that Our Lady always wants to give us, or who may never have got to know her in their faith journey, need to be "introduced to her". The Home Novena is a golden opportunity for you to make the introductions. When parents and grandparents become aware that they can offer great support to their children and grandchildren through prayer, they will jump at the opportunity. The Home Novena offers them the perfect opportunity to come together, in a small group, with people whom they know, and begin a new way of parenting – spiritual parenting, through the powerful intercession of Our Mother of Perpetual Succour.

Starting the Home Novena would surely be a fitting way to celebrate the 150th anniversary of the gift of this fountain of grace to the Church. If the Perpetual Novena is not held or has never been held in your parish church you may be able to introduce this devotion to your friends and it will become a source of great healing and comfort for them. For yourself, too, it will become a source of great blessing, a "fountain of grace" flowing in your own home. If you feel called to begin a Home Novena you will find support on our dedicated website. Go to: Mary.novena-at-home.redemptorists.co.uk.[7]

---

7   For further information or discussion email: novena-at-home@redemptorists.co.uk

— Chapter 5 —

Reading the message of the Icon of Love

You may have known and loved the icon of Our Mother of Perpetual Succour all your life, or all your adult life. But no matter how well we may know the icon it is always enlightening to look at it again and read its message afresh. Especially if you are praying with a small group in a Home Novena, it is good to be able to talk about the message, about what the icon says to you, and to ask others what the icon says to them.

An icon is not like the paintings that we are accustomed to in our Western European churches. The icon belongs to an art form that was developed many centuries ago in the Eastern European Churches, particularly in Greece and Russia and in the great city that was once named Constantinople and is now Istanbul, in Turkey. The iconographer speaks of "writing the icon", not painting it. Before religious iconographers begin the work of writing a religious icon they spend a long time in prayer and fasting. They begin by reciting this prayer:

> You,
> Divine Master of all that exists,
> illuminate and direct
> the soul, the heart and the mind
> of your servant;
> guide my hands
> that I may represent
> fittingly and with perfection
> your image, that of your Holy Mother

and that of all the saints
for the glory,
joy,
and embellishment
of your Holy Church.[1]

Writing a religious icon is a profoundly spiritual work. It was undertaken normally by monks in the silence of their monasteries. Throughout the whole composition of the icon, the iconographer seeks to live in the presence of God, to be, as it were, a pen in the hand of God with which God writes a message to God's people.

A picture is worth a thousand words

We often say that a picture is worth a thousand words. And certainly just one glance at the icon of Our Mother of Perpetual Succour is enough to instil calm in the soul. We come into the presence of one who loves us and fills us with confidence in the mercy of God. The icon proclaims the Gospel of God's love in our hearts. The very title, Our Mother of Perpetual Succour, or Perpetual Help, resonates deeply in our souls. That is who Our Lady is: she is our spiritual mother and she takes care of each one of us. Cardinal Vincent Nichols, Archbishop of Westminster, spoke personally about the effect a glance at the icon of Our Lady has on him. In his homily during the ceremony when he assumed the patronage of the church of St Alphonsus[2] and its shrine to Our Mother of Perpetual Succour he told the congregation that he had a copy of the icon in his office. And he said,

> Any time I glance at this Icon I feel better. I feel secure. I am touched deeply. Sometimes I wonder why that is so. There is, I think, a real sense of depth in this beautiful image of Mary and her child. The Icon draws us into that depth. To begin with, there is such a depth of compassion

---

1   Fabriciano Ferrero, *The Story of an Icon* (Chawton: Redemptorist Publications, 2001), p. 44.
2   Each cardinal is assigned a titular church in Rome by the Pope. Cardinal Nichols was assigned the church of St Alphonsus.

in the eyes of the Blessed Mother. She sees. She knows. She sees me. She knows me. She sees all the suffering in the world and gazes on it with such love and compassion. She sees my anxieties, my small sufferings, and helps me to see them in a true perspective. In the warmth of her compassion, I know I am not alone. I know I can bring my burden to her and, literally, leave it with her.[3]

In his beautiful cathedral at Westminster on 14 August 2014 Cardinal Nichols erected a shrine to Our Lady of Perpetual Succour. The visitor to the cathedral today – and hundreds of visitors enter the cathedral for Mass and prayer and the sacrament of reconciliation each day – sees the votive candles burning and people standing in prayer before the icon, bringing all their joys and sorrows to Our Mother of Perpetual Succour.

The icon is a presence

Anyone who looks lovingly into Our Lady's eyes in her beautiful Icon of Love can have the same experience that Cardinal Nichols has. Adelino M. Garcia Paz explains the power of an icon in this way:

In the Icon the picture is less valuable than the spiritual significance reflected in the picture. It is an original idea of the depth of Byzantine religious painting. Because of this the Orientals speak of the presence of the Spirit in the Icons. The Icon is a presence. This is most difficult to understand for the Western mentality. The Icon is the presence of Christ, of Mary, of the mystery; this presence makes us enter into communion with the person or the mystery. The Icon "reproduces" in some way, the presence of the person or mystery recalled.[4]

The icon of Our Mother of Perpetual Succour draws us into the presence of Our Lady as we pray before her image and contemplate

---

3 *Catholic Herald*, 3 October 2014.
4 Adelino M. Garcia Paz, *Holy Mary of Perpetual Help*, vol. I: *History and Interpretation of the Icon* (Singapore: Redemptorist Community, 1991), p. 78.

her in her beautiful icon. We experience her motherly love for us as she looks at us with great concern in her eyes. The icon also draws us into the presence of her child Jesus, whom she presents to us, as he clutches her thumb for comfort and support. The fright that the child Jesus experiences at the sight of the angels with the instruments of the passion reminds us vividly that the whole icon is speaking to us about the salvation that we have in Christ who has come as our redeemer, "incarnate of the Virgin Mary… [and] crucified under Pontius Pilate", as we say in the Creed.

It is Mary's loving compassion that can fill us with such great trust and joy as we look into her eyes. Even in the darkest moments, when things are not going as we would like them to go, or we are struggling with illness or anxieties about loved ones, one loving glance at Our Mother of Perpetual Succour can calm our souls and renew our hope. We can know the comfort and the assurance that the simple petition, "O Mother of Perpetual Succour, pray for me", brings us in moments of doubt or fear. The fountain of grace floods our whole being with trust as we surrender our worries to our heavenly mother.

Looking at the image

When we look at the icon we simultaneously become aware of Mary's eyes looking straight at us and her beautiful long right hand with the baby Jesus grasping her thumb in both his hands. We can't see the face of Mary without seeing the face of Jesus. We become aware, too, that the elegant fingers of Mary's right hand are pointing to Jesus. As she looks at us, with deep compassion and concern in her eyes, she is saying to us, "Look at Jesus. Don't live as if Jesus didn't matter! He matters so much that he is the way, the truth and the life." She is presenting Jesus to us and inviting us to see our saviour who will give his life for us.

As we look at the icon we see in the top corners two angels on a level with Mary's face. They are the archangels Gabriel, on the right as we view the icon, and Michael on the left. Both angels are carrying the instruments of the passion of Christ. Gabriel is carrying the cross and the nails and Michael is carrying a pot in which we see the soldier's lance and a stick with a sponge on it. While we look at the archangels we become very aware that this icon is about the passion of Jesus as well as the support that he receives from his mother. It is also about the loving and compassionate relationship that Mary wants to have with us. We see this in her face as she invites us into the mystery of her son. That is the power of the icon. We don't just stand, as it were, outside the image, admiring its artistic qualities. Rather, we feel drawn into the mystery that the icon opens up before our eyes.

When we look at Jesus we can ask ourselves, "What is Jesus looking at?" He is not looking at us, as his mother is. He is looking over his left shoulder as if he has just turned his eyes from the angel who is holding the cross and the nails. The presence of the angels, holding the instruments of the passion of the Lord, vividly focuses our attention on the passion of Jesus.

Mary's eyes

The most striking feature of the icon is Mary's eyes. Her eyes, as they look directly into our eyes, communicate the great concern she has that we follow the direction she is giving by pointing to Jesus. Her eyes proclaim that if we seek life we must go to Jesus who is our life. We also see sadness in her eyes, not the type of sadness that withdraws from life, but the sadness of a loving mother, full of compassion and concern for her children, who have many trials to overcome in this world. Her eyes look right at us without a hint of judgement or blame. This is a mother fully communicating her love and concern for all her children. Fabriciano Ferrero describes it well:

> Her face conveys the gravity of images that receive veneration. Her gaze is sacred and profound. It is

not directed towards her Son but towards whoever is contemplating her. Her large eyes with their pronounced eyebrows, her long nose, small mouth and gently pursed lips and the dark colour of her garments, give her whole figure a sacred grandeur that penetrates to the very heart of the viewer and of the mystery that she herself appears to contemplate as she gazes out.[5]

Ferrero, an expert on iconography, suggests that the best way to read the icon is to look at it slightly from the left. Then we look directly into the face of Mary. Her eyes look straight into our eyes. We also see more clearly that, as Mary looks at us, her right hand is inviting us to look at the child Jesus who has just turned away from seeing the instruments of his passion. She is pleading with us to look at her son and have compassion for what lies ahead of him.

The star

Mary is wearing a beautiful veil around her head that also covers her shoulders. At the centre of the veil, on her forehead, there is a large star with eight rays of light shining from it. A little to the left, there is a smaller cruciform star. Ferrero's comments on the meaning of the star are helpful:

> To understand the eight-pointed star that appears on the Virgin's forehead, we need to refer back to the meaning this symbol had in ancient Christian iconography. It could be said to replace "the ray of light, the hand of the Father who blesses from on high or the dove that descends bathed in light". Each of these symbolises the grace that descends upon the Mother of God.[6]

Mary is called "the morning star" and she is also called "the star of the sea". St Alphonsus, in his famous book *The Glories of Mary*, took up this tradition of seeing Mary as "star of the sea" and wrote:

---

5   Ferrero, *Story of an Icon*, p. 97.
6   Ferrero, *Story of an Icon*, p. 122.

69

Our Lady is called "The Star of the Sea" by the Church; for, as St Thomas explains it, "As mariners, in tempestuous weather, are guided by the star of the sea into port, so are souls guided by Mary over the sea of this world into paradise." Hence St Bernard warns us, saying: "If you do not wish to be lost in the storm of temptations, turn not your eyes from this star of salvation."[7]

St Alphonsus, who lived in the eighteenth century, is quoting St Thomas Aquinas, who lived in the thirteenth century, and also St Bernard, who lived in the twelfth century. The tradition of seeing Mary as "the star of the sea" began many centuries ago. And the large star on Mary's forehead in the icon still speaks to us today. Blessed Paul VI, entrusting the work of evangelisation in our time to Our Lady, prayed, "may she be the Star of the evangelization ever renewed".[8] And Pope Francis in his great apostolic exhortation *Evangelii Gaudium*, "The Joy of the Gospel", prayed to Mary with these words:

Star of the new evangelization,
help us to bear radiant witness…
that the joy of the Gospel
may reach to the ends of the earth,
illuminating even the fringes of our world.[9]

Seeing Mary as "the star of the Sea" has inspired much-loved hymns. One well-known Catholic hymn to Our Lady begins with the line, "Star of sea and ocean, gateway to God's haven". Another well-known hymn, by John Lingard, begins with the line, "Hail, Queen of heav'n, the ocean star". We have also the ancient hymn to our Lady in Latin, dating from the ninth century, *Ave maris stella* ("Hail, star of the sea"). This shows us that in popular devotion the image of Mary as "star of the sea" has a very long history, which predates the fifteenth-century icon of Our Mother of Perpetual Succour by

---

7 St Alphonsus de' Liguori, *The Glories of Mary* (London: Burns & Oates, 1852), p. 589.
8 Blessed Paul VI, *Evangelii Nuntiandi* ("Evangelisation in the Modern World"), 82.
9 Pope Francis, *Evangelii Gaudium*, 288.

many centuries. The iconographer of the miraculous icon was using images that were well known in his Church and in his community.

Mary's hands

As we gaze at the icon our attention is drawn immediately to Mary's hands. With her left hand she holds the child Jesus. And with the fingers of her right hand she points to her son, while Jesus clutches the thumb of her hand for support. She holds in her hands the one who holds the whole world in his, the eternal Word of God. As St Paul says:

> He is the image of the unseen God
> and the first-born of all creation,
> for in him were created
> all things in heaven and on earth:
> everything visible and everything invisible
> (Colossians 1:15-16).

The icon speaks to us of the mystery of the Incarnation and the divine Motherhood of Mary. It is the Son of God, made flesh in her womb by the power of the Holy Spirit, that she now nurses and supports in her hands. The Icon of Love invites us to enter into this mystery. When the angel Gabriel announced to Mary in Nazareth that she would become the mother of Jesus, he said to her, "Mary, do not be afraid; you have won God's favour," and he went on to explain to her how she would become the mother of Jesus: "The Holy Spirit will come upon you… and the power of the Most High will cover you with its shadow" (Luke 1:31. 35). Mary believed. She began to live "on every word that comes from the mouth of God" (Matthew 4:4). She was not afraid to face any situation because she believed that the power of God overshadowed her. Even at the foot of the

71

cross she will stand, suffering with her dying son, but still living by those words, "Mary, do not be afraid," and still believing what the archangel Gabriel said about her son: "He will be great and will be called Son of the Most High. The Lord God will give him the throne of his ancestor David; he will rule over the house of Jacob for ever and his reign will have no end" (Luke 1:32-33). She has the faith to trust God in every situation, no matter how hopeless it may seem. Now, as we see her holding the child Jesus in her hands, we see him trusting her and seeking comfort and protection from her.

The child Jesus

Seeing the child Jesus in Mary's hands we are invited to renew our faith in the mystery of the Incarnation. The child who takes fright at seeing the archangel Gabriel with the instruments of the passion is the son of Mary, but he is also the Son of God, consubstantial with the Father in his divinity and fully sharing in our humanity. "The Word was made flesh, he lived among us" (John 1:14) is how St John the Evangelist, who stood at the foot of the cross with Mary, describes the mystery of the Incarnation. John also tells us that "God is love" (1 John 4:8). So it is love itself that has become flesh and been born of Mary. When we see the child Jesus in Mary's arms we are seeing love itself. We can say that while the icon speaks to us of the passion of Christ it is also the Icon of Love: the love of God incarnate; the love of God poured into our hearts by the Holy Spirit; the love of Jesus who said, "A man can have no greater love than to lay down his life for his friends" (John 15:13); the love of our Blessed Mother who is so concerned that we open our hearts to receive God's love.

We can see that the child Jesus had a great fright as the archangels presented the instruments of the passion. His face is very serene and determined as he looks resolutely into the distance. One gets the impression that the face of the child has matured well beyond his tender age. Despite his terror he will face what has to be faced because, as he will proclaim when he begins preaching the Gospel,

God loved the world so much
that he gave his only Son,
so that everyone who believes in him may not be lost
but may have eternal life.
For God sent his Son into the world
not to condemn the world,
but so that through him the world might be saved
(John 3:16-17).

We can see in the resolute appearance of the child Jesus that he will fulfil his mission.

The symbol of the sandal falling from his left foot as he turns to his mother for comfort and support can be read in two different ways. The most common way is to see this as being due to the fright that the child got at the sight of the archangels. They were presenting him with the instruments of his passion, a vivid reminder of what lay ahead of him. In his fright, as the child rapidly turns to his mother for comfort and support, the sandal falls from his foot. That makes sense. It anticipates the account of his agony in the garden when his sweat fell like drops of blood. On the other hand, however, the sandal might well be a biblical symbol based on the book of Ruth where we read: "Now in former times it was the custom in Israel, in matters of redemption or exchange, to confirm the transaction by one of the parties removing his scandal and giving it to the other" (Ruth 4:7). Our redemption now is in the hands of Christ. He sees in the instruments of the passion the suffering that he will have to

73

undergo to redeem us. He willingly enters into an agreement with God and with us and presents his sandal. That is the symbol of our redemption. If we read the icon in this way we don't say that the sandal falling from his foot was due to the fright. Rather, we can say that despite the fright and even the terror of what lay ahead, Jesus offers his sandal as a symbol of his redeeming us.

Either reading of the symbol of the sandal falling from the foot of Jesus is true to the overall message of the icon.

The archangels

The figures of the archangels Michael and Gabriel fill the space in the two top corners of the icon. As you look at the icon the archangel Michael is on the left and the archangel Gabriel is on the right. We identify them by means of the letters that the iconographer inscribed by each angel: by Michael we have the Greek letters *OAPM*, abbreviation for the Greek words *O Arkhangelos Mikhael* ("the archangel Michael"); by Gabriel we have the letters *OAPG*, abbreviation for *O Arkhangelos Gabriel* ("the archangel Gabriel").[10] They are looking at Jesus with great reverence, though Jesus has turned his eyes away from them. They bow towards him, in an act of worship, as they present the instruments of the passion. They know that the passion and death of Jesus will be the greatest act of worship that can be offered to God the Father. When Jesus prayed,

in his agony in the garden, "take this cup away", God the Father sent "an angel… from heaven to give him strength" (Luke 22:42-43). The reverential awe in the faces of the angels, as they present

---

10 Ferrero, *Story of an Icon*, p. 98.

the instruments of his death, gives us the clear impression that they know that he has the strength to go through with the great work that the Father has sent him to do, namely the salvation of the human race, and that they are bowing to him in adoration.

Our Mother of Perpetual Succour

As we contemplate the icon we are invited to enter with love and confidence into the mystery of Christ. Jesus says to us, "Make your home in me, as I make mine in you" (John 15:4). It is Mary herself, as she looks at us with such compassion and love in her eyes, who is imploring us to accept his invitation and make our home in the mystery of her son. The halo around the head of the child in her arms declares to us that he is Our Lord Jesus Christ, now seated at the right hand of the Father in heaven. And the halo and light around Mary's head declare to us that she is now, body and soul, in heaven with her son. The whole icon speaks to us of the salvation that Jesus Christ has won for us and how, in God's plan for our salvation, Mary plays a central role as the Mother of God and our mother. In that great moment of our redemption, as Mary stood beneath his cross as he was dying, Jesus declared that she is the mother of all his disciples. She is our spiritual mother. St John Paul II said:

> Mary is present in the Church as the Mother of Christ, and at the same time as that Mother whom Christ, in the mystery of the Redemption, gave to humanity in the person of the Apostle John. Thus, in her new motherhood in the Spirit, Mary embraces each and every one in Christ, and embraces each and every one through the Church.[11]

We enter into the depths of the mystery of our redemption as we contemplate the Icon of Love; our hearts are filled with joy and confidence in the powerful protection and embrace of Our Lady; we give thanks to God that this miraculous icon of Our Mother of

---

11 St John Paul II, *Redemptoris Mater* ("Mother of the Redeemer"), 47.

Perpetual Succour has been venerated in the Redemptorist church of St Alphonsus in Rome since 1866, and that devotion to Our Mother of Perpetual Succour has spread throughout the Church, bringing peace and joy, confidence and courage, health and wholeness to many.

Blessed Pius IX entrusted the miraculous icon to the care of the Redemptorists at the church of St Alphonsus in Rome in 1866. He himself came and prayed fervently before the holy icon. Blessed Paul VI on the occasion of the centenary of the icon's presence in the church of St Alphonsus said to the Redemptorists: "The very expressive title of Perpetual Succour with which the Virgin is invoked summarises the teaching of the Second Vatican Council about Mary, Mother of the Church, and urges the faithful to have confidence in her."[12] St John Paul II knew how to read the Icon of Love. As he knelt at the shrine of Our Mother of Perpetual Succour in the church of St Alphonsus on 30 June 1991 he prayed:

> Oh Mother of Perpetual Succour,
> Holy Mother of the Redeemer,
> magnificent sign of hope,
> we entreat you,
> come to the aid of your people,
> who long to rise again.
> Give to all the joy
> of approaching the third millennium
> in conscious and active solidarity
> with the poorest among us,
> proclaiming in a new and valiant manner
> the Gospel of your Son,
> the foundation and summit
> of all human co-existence,
> in longing for a true peace,
> fair and lasting peace.

---

12 Adelino M. Garcia Paz, *Holy Mary of Perpetual Help*, vol. III: *Person and Practices* (Singapore: Redemptorist Community, 1991), p. 26

Like the infant Jesus,
whom we admire in this venerated icon,
we too wish to clasp your right hand.
You have the power and the goodness
to help us
in every need and situation.
This is your hour!
Come to our aid
And be the refuge and hope
of us all.
Amen.[13]

---

13   Ferrero, *Story of an Icon*, p. 20.

— Chapter 6 —

The powerful intercession of Our Mother of Perpetual Succour

We have been reflecting on how the miraculous icon of Our Mother of Perpetual Succour has become the fountain of grace for many millions of Catholics and, indeed, for many hundreds of thousands of non-Catholics and non-Christians, in the past 150 years. The word "fountain" provides us with a good image for speaking about devotion to Our Lady and about her powerful intercession on our behalf. In the days before bottled water became popular, people would go to the water fountain in their school or place of work when they needed a drink. The fountain itself is not the water, but the water will not spout without the fountain. By way of analogy, we can say the same of Our Lady and refer to devotion to Our Lady as the fountain of grace. The fountain is not the grace; Christ is the grace. But the grace of Christ "flows and spouts" when petitioners come to the fountain. The Church, in the Litany of Loreto, has many similar titles for Our Lady. She is called, just to mention a few: "Seat of wisdom"; "Spiritual vessel"; "Tower of David"; "Ark of the covenant"; "Gate of heaven".

We have seen how the miraculous Icon of Love has inspired many millions of Christians, and in some places non-Christians, to open their hearts in faith and confidence to the mother of Jesus. And Jesus, who has given us his mother to be our mother also, has blessed them with a fresh outpouring of the Holy Spirit. This is the experience of the faithful in every age and it explains why devotion to Our Lady has been a constant feature of Catholic life. The oldest traditional prayer for Mary's help, dating from the early third century, shows the confidence that God's people, in the earliest days of the Church, had in the intercession of Our Lady. We still say the same prayer today: "We fly to thy protection, O holy Mother of God, despise not our petition in our necessities, but deliver us from all danger, O ever glorious and blessed Virgin."

The Greek version of this prayer dates from the early third century. Since this prayer was already written down – and writing was not all that common in those days – the Christians of Alexandria in Egypt could have been saying this prayer from as early as the second century. Surely it is very significant that at this early stage in the development of the Church, Christians were turning with such great confidence to Our Lady and asking for her powerful intercession? That prayer has survived the centuries because Christians in every age have experienced the power of Mary's intercession. In this final chapter I want to discuss how the Catholic Church has always seen the intercessory role of Mary our mother in the work of our redemption. Mary is not absent from the Church nor from the experience of the faithful.

Jesus the redeemer and Mary the intercessor[1]

St Teresa of Avila, a Doctor of the Church, wrote:

> It is clear to me that if we wish to please God and to receive graces in abundance from him, it is God's will that these graces should come to us through the hands of Christ in his most holy humanity, that humanity in which his Majesty has proclaimed that he is well pleased. Apart from the fact that God himself has told me this, time and time again I have noticed it in my own experience; I say it again, I have seen with my own eyes that it is by this door that we must enter if we wish his Supreme Majesty to reveal to us great and hidden mysteries.[2]

---

1   The material in the next few pages, on Mary's intercessory role, is based on material that first appeared in Jim McManus, *All Generations Will Call Me Blessed: Mary at the Millennium* (Chawton: Redemptorist Publications, 2007).

2   Office of Readings, 15 October.

St Teresa has clearly stated the Church's teaching on Christ as the source of all our graces. All the graces of our salvation come to us through Christ. Jesus Christ in his sacred humanity is our one mediator with the Father. But his birth as our redeemer was due to the consent and cooperation of Mary, his mother. Her maternal cooperation with her son didn't cease with his birth. She mothered him through his childhood and adolescence and accompanied him throughout his life, even to Calvary. As the Second Vatican Council said, "Thus, in a very special way [Mary] cooperated by her obedience, faith, hope and burning charity in the work of the Saviour in restoring supernatural life to souls. For this reason she is a mother to us in the order of grace."[3] Our restoration to grace was entirely the work of Christ, but Mary's cooperation with him has left a Marian imprint on our salvation. The grace of salvation, which comes entirely from Christ, has a maternal aspect. St John Paul II wrote:

> And so, in the redemptive economy of grace, brought about through the action of the Holy Spirit, there is a unique correspondence between the moment of the Incarnation of the Word and the moment of the birth of the Church. The person who links these two moments is Mary: Mary at Nazareth and Mary in the Upper Room at Jerusalem. In both cases her discreet yet essential presence indicates the path of "birth from the Holy Spirit." Thus, she who is present in the mystery of Christ as Mother becomes – by the will of her Son and the power of the Holy Spirit – present in the mystery of the Church. In the Church too she continues to be a maternal presence.[4]

Mary is not just a *memory* in the Church. She is not just some great woman that once lived on earth. She is our real, living, loving, caring Mother of Perpetual Succour. She knows each one of us and is concerned for each one of us. Her maternal presence in our daily lives takes an intercessory form. According to the Second Vatican Council:

---

3   *Lumen Gentium*, Dogmatic Constitution on the Church, 61.
4   St John Paul II, *Redemptoris Mater* ("Mother of the Redeemer"), 24.

This motherhood of Mary in the order of grace continues without interruption from the consent which she loyally gave at the Annunciation and which she sustained without wavering beneath the cross, until the eternal consummation of all the elect.[5]

Mediation of intercession

The Church, then, clearly believes that just as Mary played an active role in the life and work of Jesus, so she plays an active role in the life and work of his disciples, his Church, which is his mystical body in our world. Mary is present in the Church as our sister, but also as our spiritual mother. As the Second Vatican Council said, "By her motherly love she cares for her Son's sisters and brothers who still journey on earth surrounded by dangers and difficulties, until they are led into their blessed home."[6] Her maternal care is exercised through her intercession with her son on our behalf. This does not imply that Jesus himself doesn't care or that he needs his mother to remind him to care, or that we cannot approach Jesus directly ourselves. It means that Jesus honours his mother who was chosen by God the Father to be his mother and who was also chosen by God the Father to be the spiritual mother of all the disciples of Jesus, the mother of the Church.

The wedding feast at Cana

We see Jesus honouring his mother at Cana, when he responded to her request and provided wine for the wedding feast. But when we listen to the story of Jesus changing the water into wine we must remind ourselves that the abundance of wine has a profound symbolic meaning. It is the sign of God's kingdom. It is also a sign of Our Lady's intercessory and maternal role in the kingdom of God.

We will reflect on this Gospel story in some detail because as we listen to it we see more profoundly the intercessory role of Mary.

---

5   *Lumen Gentium*, 62.
6   *Lumen Gentium*, 62.

We could ask the question, why does John the Evangelist begin his account of the Lord's public ministry by telling the story of the wedding feast at Cana? What has a wedding feast got to do with the Good News, with the work of our redemption? At the end of his Gospel John tells us,

> There were many other signs that Jesus worked and the disciples saw, but they are not recorded in this book. These are recorded so that you may believe that Jesus is the Christ, the Son of God, and that believing this you may have life through his name (John 20:30-31).

John is telling us that he includes the wedding feast story so that we may believe that Jesus is the Christ. It is not just an act of kindness on Jesus' part. It is a revelation of who Jesus is. And Jesus gave this revelation in response to a request from his mother. Let's consider the story in this light.

The evangelist writes,

> Three days later there was a wedding at Cana in Galilee. The mother of Jesus was there, and Jesus and his disciples had also been invited (John 2:1).

Mary, as she is mentioned first in the guest list, is the principal guest. Wedding feasts in those days could last the whole week. The provision of wine for the feast was the responsibility of the bridegroom. At this wedding in Cana something had gone badly wrong. We are told,

> When they ran out of wine, since the wine provided for the wedding was all finished, the mother of Jesus said to him, "They have no wine". Jesus said, "Woman, why turn to me? My hour has not come yet" (John 2:3-4).

Jesus seems to be responding to a different statement. Mary seems to be talking about the acutely embarrassing situation in which the young married couple find themselves. Jesus, however, by mentioning "my hour", seems to be referring to the hour of his death on the cross.

Despite what appears to us as Jesus' apparent refusal to get involved in the embarrassing situation of the lack of wine in Cana, Mary is confident that Jesus will respond to her request. She doesn't hear any refusal in his response. She says to the servants, "Do whatever he tells you." She is expecting him to act. And she is not disappointed. Jesus tells the servants to fill the six stone water jars that could each hold twenty or thirty gallons with water. Then he says,

> "Draw some out now and take it to the steward." They did this; the steward tasted the water, and it had turned into wine… the steward called the bridegroom and said, "People generally serve the best wine first, and keep the cheaper sort till the guests have had plenty to drink; but you have kept the best wine till now" (John 2:8-10).

In response to his mother's request, Jesus not only provided enough wine for the wedding party in Cana, he also provided the prophet Isaiah's symbol of salvation in creating an abundance of wine (Isaiah 25:6): over a thousand bottles of the "best wine"! St John says,

> This was the first of the signs given by Jesus: it was given at Cana in Galilee. He let his glory be seen, and his disciples believed in him (John 2:11).

The abundance of wine was not a sign that Jesus could work miracles. It was a sign that the kingdom of God was at hand. That is why in performing this sign Jesus "let his glory be seen", his glory as the Messiah, the saviour, and also why "his disciples believed in him". They didn't simply believe because Jesus produced an abundance of wine for the wedding party in Cana. They believed in Jesus as the Messiah, because they saw in that abundance of wine the prophetic sign of the coming of the kingdom.

In the Old Testament God's redemption of God's people is spoken of in terms of a wedding feast: "Like a young man marrying a virgin, so will the one who built you wed you, and as the bridegroom rejoices in his bride, so will your God rejoice in you" (Isaiah 62:5). For other references to this biblical theme of the messianic nuptials, see Hosea 2:16-25; Jeremiah 2:1-2; 3:1. 6-12; Ezekiel 16; Isaiah 50:1; 54:4-8. The Lord's covenant with his people is symbolised as a nuptial union. Jesus himself uses the symbol of the wedding feast to speak about the kingdom: "The kingdom of heaven may be compared to a king who gave a feast for his son's wedding..." (Matthew 22:1-14). On the symbolic level, then, we have to understand the wedding feast as the place where revelation will take place, where faith will be shared because the wedding feast itself is the sign of the new nuptials between God and God's people, the sign of the new covenant that Christ will establish and proclaim when he takes the cup at the Last Supper, when "his hour" has come, and he says, "This cup is the new covenant in my blood which will be poured out for you" (Luke 22:20).

Woman

The wedding feast at Cana is a symbol of the nuptials of the new covenant. That is why John doesn't tell us anything about any of the other guests, not even the bride. John is not really interested in the bride and groom and the other guests. The only names on his guest list are Mary and Jesus and Jesus' disciples. The wedding feast is the symbolic background to "the first of the signs given by Jesus". Mary and her intervention with Jesus are at the centre of this first sign. Jesus himself draws our attention to the centrality of Mary by addressing her not as "Mother" but as "Woman". Raymond Brown points out that in the whole of the Bible and ancient literature there is not a single example, apart from Cana and Calvary, of a son addressing his mother as "Woman".[7] In addressing her thus Jesus

---

7   Raymond E. Brown, *The Gospel According to John*, Anchor Bible 29 (Garden City, NY: Doubleday, 1966), 1:99.

is drawing our attention to something new, something different about his mother and about their relationship. Ignace de la Potterie explains it in this way:

> We have to keep in mind that from this moment on Jesus "begins" to *manifest himself* as Messiah and, by that very fact, the relationship between him and Mary is no longer the same; it is no longer the simple relationship of a son to his mother. Jesus now takes upon himself another role (a messianic role); and, what is very important, in addressing his mother as "Woman," he *involves her* in his mission, which is beginning. By this appellation, he places a certain distance between himself and their former relationship, that of mother-son, but at the same time, he opens up a new perspective; and he entices her into accepting another relationship with him in the mystery of salvation, beyond the maternal and familial.[8]

Mary is not just the biological mother of Jesus. She has become his disciple. Indeed, as Blessed Paul VI said, "She was the first and the most perfect of Christ's disciples."[9] And St John Paul II wrote,

> In a sense Mary as Mother became the first "disciple" of her Son, the first to whom he seemed to say: "Follow me", even before he addressed this call to the Apostles or to anyone else.[10]

It is as his "first 'disciple'" that Mary hears Jesus address her as "Woman". From her response to being addressed as "Woman" we can see that she entered wholeheartedly into this master–disciple relationship. Jesus, her Messiah and her son, has called her and she will follow all the way to Calvary where Jesus will once again address her as "Woman" when he proclaims her the mother of the disciple.

---

8   Ignace de la Potterie, *Mary in the Mystery of the Covenant* (Staten Island: Alba House, 1992), p. 202.
9   Blessed Paul VI, *Marialis Cultus* ("To Honour Mary"), 35.
10 St John Paul II, *Redemptoris Mater*, 20.

Mary went to the servants at the wedding feast and said to them, "Do whatever he tells you." Despite our difficulties in understanding Jesus' enigmatic expression, "Woman, why turn to me? My hour has not come yet," we see that Mary understood this in such a way that she immediately began to prepare the "servants" to obey the instructions of Jesus. Indeed, scholars point out that the words Mary uses – "Do whatever he tells you" – are very similar to the words the people of Israel used when they committed themselves to the covenant with God: "All that the Lord has said, we will do" (Exodus 19:8). Mary, recalling the people's profession of faith in the old covenant, now exhorts the "servants" to have the same attitude towards Jesus that their ancestors had towards the God of the covenant. Mary is already exercising her spiritual motherhood and preparing the servants, the disciples, to have complete trust in Jesus. She herself has become the first disciple of her son as he assumes his messianic role. The Anglican–Roman Catholic International Commission highlights the change in Mary's relationship with Jesus in this way:

> Mary's response, to instruct the servants to "Do whatever he tells you" (2:5), is unexpected; she is not in charge of the feast (cf. 2:8). Her initial role as the mother of Jesus has radically changed. She herself is now seen as a believer within the messianic community. From this moment on, she commits herself totally to the Messiah and his word. A new relationship results, indicated by the change in the order of the main characters at the end of the story: "After this he went down to Capernaum, with his mother and his brothers and his disciples" (2:12). The Cana narrative opens by placing Jesus within the family of Mary, his mother; from now on, Mary is part of the "company of Jesus", his disciple. Our reading of this passage reflects the Church's understanding of the role of Mary: to help the disciples come to her son, Jesus Christ, and to "do whatever he tells you".[11]

---

11 Anglican–Roman Catholic International Commission, *Mary: Grace and Hope in Christ* (2004), 25.

Jesus is the bridegroom

When we see Cana in this light, the behaviour of Mary and Jesus begins to make sense. They actually took over. The young couple are well in the background. Mary takes the initiative, approaches Jesus and then gives orders to the servants. Jesus reminds his mother that his hour has not yet come and then he too gives orders to the servants – and all this without the knowledge of the couple. Why have Mary and Jesus taken over the running of the feast? Because, in John's Gospel, the real feast is the messianic one, where Jesus is the bridegroom and the Church is his bride. This understanding was well expressed by St Bernard in the Middle Ages when he wrote:

> This was a great sign of the divine force and power to change water into wine solely by his will. But in this miracle another change is significant for us, which is also a work of the finger of God: and this is so much the better and more salutary for us: we are all called to the spiritual wedding feast where Jesus Christ, our Lord, is the Bridegroom.[12]

In John's Gospel, John the Baptist calls Jesus "the bridegroom" (3:29). Jesus is the true bridegroom at the messianic wedding. His transforming presence effects not just the physical miracle of changing the water into wine but the symbolic miracle of changing the water into the life-giving wine of the new covenant. That abundant supply of the miraculous "best wine" is a sign to his disciples. John says, "He let his glory be seen, and his disciples believed in him."

Jesus claimed that role of "bridegroom" for himself. We read in the Gospel:

> One day when John's disciples and the Pharisees were fasting, some people came and said to him, "Why is it that John's disciples and the disciples of the Pharisees

---

12 St Bernard, cited by de la Potterie, *Mary in the Mystery of the Covenant*, p. 200.

fast, but your disciples do not?" Jesus replied, "Surely the bridegroom's attendants would never think of fasting while the bridegroom is still with them? As long as they have the bridegroom with them, they could not think of fasting. But the time will come for the bridegroom to be taken away from them, and then, on that day, they will fast" (Mark 2:18-20).

On these verses Benedict XVI wrote:

Jesus identifies himself here as the "bridegroom" of God's promised marriage with his people and, by doing so, he mysteriously places his own existence, himself, within the mystery of God. In him, in an unexpected way, God and man become one, become a "marriage", though this marriage – as Jesus subsequently points out – passes through the Cross, through the "taking away" of the bridegroom.[13]

The symbol of wine

If we stay just on the surface of the Cana story we can miss the deeper symbolism of the "wedding feast" and the significance of the exchange between Mary and Jesus. Lack of wine is the symbol in the prophet Isaiah of the people's need and yearning for salvation:

There is lamentation in the streets: no wine,
joy quite gone,
gladness banished from the country (Isaiah 24:11).

Does Jesus hear in his mother's observation, "They have no wine," a reference to the urgent need of salvation for the people? If he does, his response, "My hour has not come yet," makes sense. He will have to await the hour of his death and resurrection to bring that salvation. But, because the abundance of wine is the prophet's symbol of redemption, Jesus can anticipate his redemptive death

---

13 Benedict XVI, *Jesus of Nazareth* (London: Bloomsbury, 2007), vol. I, p. 252.

by providing, at his mother's request, the symbol of redemption. The prophet said:

> The Lord of hosts will prepare for all peoples
> a banquet of rich food, a banquet of fine wines,
> of food rich and juicy, of fine strained wines.
> On this mountain he will remove
> the mourning veil covering all peoples,
> and the shroud enwrapping all nations,
> he will destroy Death for ever (Isaiah 25:6-7).

Since Jesus is the bridegroom at the messianic wedding feast we have to reread the story of the wedding feast at Cana in the light of the prophecy of Amos: "The mountains will run with new wine and the hills all flow with it" (Amos 9:13). The wedding at Cana is about the new wine of salvation that Jesus, the divine bridegroom, brings, and he brings it in response to his mother's request.

John the Baptist had identified Jesus as "the bridegroom" when he said, "The bride is only for the bridegroom" (John 3:29). In scripture, God's people are the bride and God himself is the bridegroom. The prophet Hosea wrote, "When that day comes – it is the Lord who speaks – she will call me 'My husband', no longer will she call me, 'My Baal'" (Hosea 2:18). And the prophet Isaiah said, "For now your creator will be your husband, his name, the Lord of hosts" (Isaiah 54:5). Because of this marriage union between God and God's people, sin is referred to in scripture as the breaking of the marriage vow, as adultery.

The specific mission of Jesus, the divine bridegroom, is "to save his people from their sins" (Matthew 1:21). Jesus is the bridegroom and the Church is his bride. In providing the abundance of wine, the wine of salvation, for the wedding feast in Cana at the beginning of his public ministry, Jesus shows that God's salvation is at hand. He let his glory be seen as the divine bridegroom, bringing salvation to his bride, and that is why his disciples believed in him. As one scripture scholar observes, "When the mother of Jesus says to him, 'They have no wine', she places him in the role of the bridegroom, whose responsibility it is to provide the wine."[14]

We see in the abundance of wine that Jesus, the bridegroom of God's people, provided for the wedding feast the symbol of God's kingdom. God the "Father of mercies" is fulfilling God's promise to redeem God's people. We see also that Jesus anticipated his "hour", at his mother's request, by providing the prophetic sign of wine in abundance and assuming his role as the "bridegroom" of God's people. Jesus responds to his mother's request with an abundance of the best wine. Mary's intercession with her son is just as powerful today for us as it was for that married couple in Cana at the beginning of the Gospel. Whenever we bring our problems and our needs to Our Lady, she will say to Jesus, "They have no wine"! That is why we call her Our Mother of Perpetual Succour, of perpetual intercession for us her children.

Reflecting on the wedding in Cana, St John Paul II wrote:

> The description of the Cana event outlines what is actually manifested as a new kind of motherhood according to the spirit and not just according to the flesh, that is to say Mary's solicitude for human beings, her coming to them in the wide variety of their wants and needs. At Cana in Galilee there is shown only one concrete aspect of human need, apparently a small one of little importance ("They have no wine"). But it has a symbolic value: this coming to the aid of human needs means, at the same time, bringing those needs within the radius of Christ's messianic mission and salvific power. Thus there is a mediation: Mary places herself between her Son and mankind in the reality of their wants, needs and sufferings. She puts herself "in the middle," that is to say she acts as a mediatrix not as an

---

14 Brant Pitre, *Jesus the Bridegroom* (New York: Image, 2014), p. 45.

outsider, but in her position as mother. She knows that as such she can point out to her Son the needs of mankind, and in fact she "has the right" to do so. Her mediation is thus in the nature of intercession: Mary "intercedes" for mankind.[15]

Mary's new role honoured by Jesus

Jesus accepts his mother's new role as our mother; he honours her concerns for us; he welcomes her as his mother when she brings our needs into "the radius of his messianic mission and power"; he welcomes her "mediation of intercession". That is the theological basis of Mary's mediation. Mary's intercession with Jesus is not a substitute for Jesus' intercession with the Father. Her intercession is on the level of her motherhood, whereas Jesus' intercession is on the level of his divine Sonship and his redemptive obedience. While Jesus stands before the Father, as our high priest, offering himself for our salvation, Mary stands before Jesus as his mother, interceding for us who have become her children through his word from the cross.

Mary's spiritual motherhood is Christ's gift to us; her maternal intercession and mediation for us are Christ's gift to her as the spiritual mother of all the disciples. When he said to his mother, "Woman, this is your son" (John 19:26), he commissioned her to take care of all his disciples, and he endowed her with the grace of intercession for this task. The one mediator between God and us, Jesus Christ, gave his mother the grace of spiritual motherhood of all the faithful. Mary's mediation of intercession never takes the place of Christ's mediation of redemption. The Second Vatican Council said:

> Mary's function as mother of humankind in no way obscures or diminishes this unique mediation of Christ, but rather shows its power. All the Blessed Virgin's salutary influence on men and women originates not in any inner necessity but in the disposition of God. It flows forth from

15   St John Paul II, *Redemptoris Mater*, 21.

the superabundance of the merits of Christ, rests on his mediation, depends entirely on it and draws all its power from it. It does not hinder in any way the immediate union of the faithful with Christ but on the contrary fosters it.[16]

This ecumenically sensitive statement is a clear expression of the Catholic belief in Mary's "mediation of intercession". The Marian titles of "Mediatrix of All Graces" or "Co-Redemptrix", which some hoped would be defined by the Second Vatican Council, were not developed by the Council Fathers. Pius XII had received many requests for a dogmatic definition of Mary's mediation as "Co-Redemptrix" or "Mediatrix of All Graces". No one could accuse that great pope of being a minimalist in Marian teaching and devotion, yet he felt that this type of emphasis on Mary's mediation was not yet theologically clear enough or mature enough for such a definition.

Vatican II agreed with him. One of the great debates in the Council concerned how to treat Mary. Some bishops wanted the Council to publish a separate document on Mary; others wanted the role of Mary to be discussed in the context of the Church. When the matter was put to a vote in the Council, the proposal that the role of Mary should be treated in the document on the Church was carried by a very slim majority, 1,114 to 1,074. Chapter VIII of the Council's Constitution on the Church is devoted to Our Lady. Here we find the authentic teaching of the Church on Mary and on her role in the history of our salvation. At the close of the Third Session of the Council on 21 November 1964 Blessed Paul VI solemnly proclaimed Mary to be the "Mother of the Church": "For the glory of the Virgin and our consolation, we proclaim Mary the Most Holy Mother of the Church, that is, the Mother of the whole People of God, both the faithful and the pastors."

Great saints and doctors of the church have preached about Mary being the mediatrix of all graces. St Bernard said, "God wills us

---

16 *Lumen Gentium*, 60.

to have everything through Mary." The influential books *The True Devotion* by St Louis Grignion de Montfort and *The Glories of Mary* by St Alphonsus Liguori are based on the conviction that we receive all grace through Mary's mediation. When the Council failed to take up this belief in a more positive way and promote the understanding of Mary as our mediatrix, many Catholics were disappointed. The Council, as quoted above, clearly stated the nature of Mary's mediation: "It flows forth from the superabundance of the merits of Christ, rests on his mediation, depends entirely on it and draws all its power from it." Mary's mediation is always subordinate to and dependent on the mediation of Christ. But Mary's mediation is real, it is efficacious, it is maternal. She is Our Mother of Perpetual Succour. That is why the Second Vatican Council said,

> The church does not hesitate to profess this subordinate role of Mary, which it constantly experiences and recommends to the heartfelt attention of the faithful, so that encouraged by this maternal help they may the more closely adhere to the Mediator and Redeemer.[17]

Because Mary is our spiritual mother and mediates with her son on our behalf, the Church has always sought her powerful intercession. Mary's mediation is, in the words of St John Paul II, "a mediation of intercession". We do not say that no grace will be given if Mary doesn't ask; rather, we say that every grace for which Mary asks will be granted. She is our loving mother, always seeking our eternal salvation. Mary continues to intercede for us, even if we never ask for her intercession. She asks Jesus for all the graces we need. Hence we can say that every grace we receive comes to us through the intercession of Mary our mother. There is no grace that we need for which she doesn't ask. That's what mothers do. They ask for all good things for their children. Mary's intercession with Jesus is all-powerful because she only asks according to the will of God. She knows that God wills each one of us to be saved. That is

---

17 *Lumen Gentium*, 62.

why she continually asks for all the graces we need to secure our eternal salvation. And that is why we rejoice in honouring her as Our Mother of Perpetual Succour.

Conclusion

We witnessed the power of Our Lady's intercession at work when, on 26 April 1866, a providential fountain of grace was opened for the universal Church. The miraculous icon of Our Mother of Perpetual Succour, which had been lost and forgotten for many years, was solemnly enshrined in the Redemptorist church of St Alphonsus in Rome. We have been amazed at how this miraculous icon of Our Lady, unknown to the Church and the world in 1865, had become, within a few decades, known, loved and cherished throughout the Catholic world. We witnessed an amazing religious phenomenon in the globalisation of devotion to Our Mother of Perpetual Succour on all the continents of the world. Mary's powerful intercession guided pastoral leaders to develop the format of the Perpetual Novena to make it possible for the devotees of Our Lady, throughout most of the twentieth century, to come together in their millions to pray for her powerful protection.

Now in this twenty-first century we can be confident that the novena devotions will continue to be a source of healing and encouragement for the millions who make the novena each year. We can also be confident that new forms of the novena devotions will evolve, especially in those places where churches no longer have the novena, ensuring that this fountain of grace will continue to flow copiously for God's people. The whole family, parents and grandparents, aunts and uncles, will always need the opportunity to come together in faith to pray for their children and grandchildren, their nieces and nephews. In their turn, children and grandchildren welcome the opportunity to pray to Our Lady for their parents and grandparents. And, as the family prays, they will continue to experience, as millions have experienced in the past 150 years, that miracles do happen through the powerful intercession of Our Mother of Perpetual Succour. We give thanks for the fountain of grace, the Icon of Love with which God has blessed the Church and the world.

— Appendix —

The Novena Prayers to Our Mother of Perpetual Succour

Beginning with the sign of the cross the leader says:

Let us unite with Christians of all ages in praising Mary and committing ourselves to her powerful protection.

We fly to your patronage, O holy Mother of God, despise not our petitions in our necessities, but deliver us from all dangers, O glorious and blessed Virgin.
Pray for us, O holy Mother of God:
That we may be made worthy of the promises of Christ.

Let us pray.

Lord Jesus Christ, you have given us your Mother, Mary, to be our Mother, ready at every moment to help us: grant, as we pray before her image and call on her help, that we may always be faithful to the graces that are ours through your death and resurrection. May the life they bring us be to your glory on earth and our eternal happiness in heaven. Amen.

Scripture reading

A short passage of scripture is read. It is recommended that the reader reads this passage slowly and then those present pause for a time to ponder the word in their hearts. The reading could be from the preceding Sunday Gospel.

Magnificat

Having pondered the word in our hearts we can then respond with the words Mary herself used when she responded to the words of her cousin, Elizabeth:

My soul glorifies the Lord,
my spirit rejoices in God, my Saviour.
He looks on his servant in her lowliness;
henceforth all ages will call me blessed.
The Almighty works marvels for me.
Holy is his name!
His mercy is from age to age,
on those who fear him.
He puts forth his arm in strength
and scatters the proud-hearted.
He casts the mighty from their thrones
and raises the lowly.
He fills the starving with good things,
sends the rich away empty.
He protects Israel, his servant,
remembering his mercy,
the mercy promised to our fathers,
to Abraham and his sons for ever.
Glory be to the Father and to the Son and to the Holy Spirit.
As it was in the beginning, is now, and ever shall be, world without end. Amen.

Let us pray.

Holy Mother of God, Virgin ever-blessed, O Mary Immaculate, pray for us, intercede for us, do not refuse to help us. We are confident, and know for certain, that you can obtain all you will from your son, our Lord Jesus Christ, the King of ages, who lives with the Father and the Holy Spirit, for ever and ever. Amen.

Our petitions

We now bring all our petitions to Our Lady, privately or inviting the others to keep particular needs in their prayers. Especially while praying for those who are sick or in trouble of one kind or another, the prayer of the community is very helpful. We remember that we are asking not just through the prayers of those in our little Home Novena group but that we are uniting with the prayers of the faithful all over the world. So we can pray with great confidence.

Prayers for the novena

Lord Jesus Christ, at a word from Mary, your Mother, you changed water into wine at Cana of Galilee. Listen to your people gathered to honour Our Mother of Perpetual Succour. Grant our petitions and accept our humble thanks.

O Mother of Perpetual Succour, we call upon your most powerful name. You are the safeguard of the living and the salvation of the dying. Your name will always be on our lips, especially in time of temptation and at the hour of our death. Your name is confidence and power. Blessed Lady, help us whenever we call on you. We will not be satisfied with merely pronouncing your name. Our daily lives will proclaim that you are truly our Mother of Perpetual Succour.

Remember, O most gracious Virgin Mary, that never was it known that anyone who fled to your protection, implored your help, or sought your intercession, was left unaided. Inspired with this confidence, I fly unto you, O Virgin of virgins, my mother. To you I come, before you I stand, sinful and sorrowful. Mother of the Word Incarnate, despise not my petitions, but in your mercy hear and answer me. Amen.

You have been made for us, O Lady, a refuge,
a helper in need and tribulation.

Let us pray.

Almighty and merciful Lord, you have given us to venerate the picture of your most blessed Mother under the special title of Perpetual Succour.

Graciously grant that, amidst the changes of our journey through life, we may be so defended by the continual protection of the same Immaculate and Ever-Virgin Mary that we may deserve to obtain the rewards of your eternal redemption, who live and reign with the Father and the Holy Spirit, world without end. Amen.

The following prayer is also popular as a novena prayer:

O Mother of Perpetual Succour, with the greatest of confidence we come before your holy picture to be inspired by the example of your life. We think of you at that moment when, full of faith and trust, you accepted God's call to be the mother of his Son. Help us, your children, to accept with joy our calling in life.

When you learned that your cousin, Elizabeth, was in need, you immediately went to serve her and offer her your help. Help us, like you, to be concerned with others.

We think of you at the foot of the cross. Your heart must have bled to see your son in agony. But your joy was great when he rose from the dead, victorious over the power of evil.

Mother of Sorrows, help us through our trials and disappointments. Help us not to lose heart. May we share with you and your son the joy of having courageously faced up to all the challenges of life. Amen.

Concluding prayers

Before the concluding prayer the leader of the group thanks everyone for coming and joining in the prayer. He or she may invite anyone present who wants to share some experience of grace with the group to do so. Then the novena concludes with everyone joining in: "Glory be to the Father and to the Son and to the Holy Spirit". It would also be appropriate to sing a hymn in honour of Our Lady at this stage.